GET UP, BABY!

*My Seven Decades with
the St. Louis Cardinals*

Mike Shannon

with Rick Hummel

TRIUMPH
B O O K S

Library of Congress Cataloging-in-Publication Data

Names: Shannon, Mike. | Hummel, Rick, author.
Title: Get up, Baby!: my seven decades with the St. Louis Cardinals / Mike Shannon, with Rick Hummel.
Identifiers: LCCN 2022005268 | ISBN 9781629379869 (Hardcover)
Subjects: LCSH: Shannon, Mike | Baseball players—United States—Biography. | Sportscasters—United States—Biography. | St. Louis Cardinals (Baseball team)—History. | Radio broadcasting of sports—Missouri—St. Louis—History.
Classification: LCC GV865.S44 A3 2022 | DDC 796.357092 [B]—dc23/eng/20220224
LC record available at https://lccn.loc.gov/2022005268

This book is available in quantity at special discounts for your group or organization. For further information, contact:
    Triumph Books LLC
    814 North Franklin Street
    Chicago, Illinois 60610
    (312) 337-0747
    www.triumphbooks.com

Printed in U.S.A.
ISBN: 978-1-62937-986-9
Design by Patricia Frey

Photos courtesy of AP Images unless otherwise indicated.

To my brother, Steve, who always
cheered for me no matter what.
—M.S.

To my wife, Melissa, who urged me to
undertake this project and kept encouraging
me when I felt I was falling behind.
—R.H.

Contents

Foreword

D ear Reader,

It's possible you live in Tacoma, Washington, or Bangor, Maine, and have never set foot in St. Louis or anywhere within the considerable reach of KMOX radio. It's possible you root only for the Seattle Mariners or Boston Red Sox and couldn't care less about the Cardinals. And, yet, somehow you have purchased this book. Possible but unlikely. Because caring about, understanding, and truly appreciating Mike Shannon is a St. Louis thing. It's a Cardinals thing. It's one of those "If you don't get it, no explanation is possible" and "If you do, none is really necessary" things.

Mike Shannon is not a national treasure. He is a Cardinals Nation treasure.

Born and raised in St. Louis. Multi-sport star at CBC High School. Recruited to play quarterback at Mizzou. Good enough that Hall of Fame coach Frank Broyles once declared that if young Mike had stuck with football, he might've won the Heisman Trophy.

Yeah, maybe. But this we know for certain. Mike chose baseball and made it to the big leagues in the early '60s in time to be a teammate of Stan Musial, whose greatest-of-all Cardinals career began in 1941. Thus, with Mike's half-century broadcasting career taking him through 2021, with a single one-degree-of-separation move, he is connected to 80 uninterrupted years of Cardinals baseball. During that time he played in three World Series and homered in each of them. In addition to Musial, Mike played with Hall of Famers Bob Gibson, Lou Brock, Orlando Cepeda, Joe Torre, Ted Simmons, and Steve Carlton, and for Hall of Famer Red Schoendienst.

When illness cut his playing career short, Mike transitioned to the broadcast booth, and that's where things really got interesting. Seated alongside Jack Buck, among broadcasting's greatest of the great, Mike was…how shall we put this? Unpolished. Early on, the bloopers and malaprops were as amusing and endearing as they were legendary—including one about a foul ball landing in the box seats and splashing into a female fan's beer. I will refrain from filling in the rest of the blanks. And maybe the story is apocryphal (game tapes weren't routinely saved back then). But that's the thing about apocryphal stories. They ring true because they could be true.

And more important, Mike was always true—to himself. Working with Jack and later Joe Buck—and with smooth pros like Ken Wilson, Bob Carpenter, Jay Randolph, Bob Starr, and John Rooney—Mike never tried to be, nor pretended to be, what they were. And over the years, from a pure broadcasting standpoint, Mike didn't just get better; he became really good. On his own terms. Listen to some of the calls: Brummer stealing home, McGwire hitting 62 and then eight more, Pujols' last-ditch homer in Houston in 2005. Those calls, and so many others, aren't good; they're great. And they are distinctively Mike Shannon.

Big moments aside, game-to-game, season-to-season, there were the reliable Shannonisms "Old Abner has done it again" or, as a long fly ball died on the warning track, "Another slab of bacon on that boy's breakfast and that baseball would have been out of here." This observation or that punctuated of course by the Shannon chuckle, "Heh Heh Heh…"

Permit me here a personal favorite. Sometime in the late '90s Mike was commenting on how the ball was really carrying that night at Busch Stadium. "In batting practice, baseballs were heading out of here like they had a date with…" A pause of several seconds ensued as Mike searched for a way to complete his thought, finally landing on…"like it had a date with...you know who." Of course. Endearing and enduring and part of the soundtrack of decades of St. Louis baseball.

At the heart of it was always this: Mike Shannon knew and loved baseball. He didn't prepare the way some of us did. He didn't have to. He brought his deep knowledge of the game itself; his long history with the Cardinals; and what he picked up at the batting cage or in the clubhouse from players, managers, and coaches who trusted him. Once in the booth, all he relied on was a simple lineup card and what he saw unfolding on the field below. His broadcasts were filled with baseball insights dispensed in his own inimitable (though comics tried) style.

The relationship between a longtime local baseball announcer and his audience is unique in sports broadcasting. Especially now, when with so much player movement, the voice of a team can be a comforting constant. The best network announcers are respected, admired, and appreciated. But the local guys—especially in baseball because of its everyday nature—and if they possess certain qualities, they can become beloved local institutions. They're regarded as part of a fan's extended family, an important part of the way baseball connects generations. It can work that way for classic announcers like Vin Scully with the Los Angeles Dodgers, Ernie Harwell with the Detroit Tigers, or Jon Miller with the San Francisco Giants. And it works in its own way with a former player who wore the uniform of the home team and then exchanged his glove for a microphone. Joe Nuxhall in Cincinnati. Herb Score in Cleveland. Jerry Remy in Boston. For these guys, as for Mike, the authentic, long-standing bond with the franchise, the undisguised rooting interest, and yes, their colorful quirks and imperfections are part of the appeal.

Over time, the audience got a good sense of Mike Shannon the person—often from the bemused and amazed testimony of his colleagues. We marveled at how day after day, night after night, through the oppressive heat and humidity of a St. Louis summer, Mike had a uniform of his own: black slacks, black shirt, black Members Only jacket. Hey, it worked for him.

Just as Babe Ruth called everybody, "Kid" (mostly because he couldn't remember their names), Mike referred to just about everybody as "Big Boy." He called me that, and I'm 5'6" and 145.

He had been an outstanding athlete. Yes, but beyond that, well into middle age and beyond, the man was a physical marvel. He seemed to need only about three hours sleep a night. If that. A game could go 15 innings and end post-midnight, and he would still be on the first tee at 7:00 AM and still show up at the booth unfazed in time for the first pitch of that afternoon's game.

Mike loved the horses. Whether an unremarkable slate at Fairmount Park or Derby Day at Churchill Downs, he wanted to be there. And don't ask me how he managed to be in Louisville for the Kentucky Derby and then back in St. Louis by the fourth or fifth inning of that night's game, but he did. The pace he maintained and the energy he brought to all of it was astounding. By the standards of most mortals, he was playing with house money from about age 40 on. And enjoying every minute of it. He's that rare person who is completely comfortable in his own skin 100 percent of the time.

Mike was a good storyteller. And a good audience when you were the one telling the story. That was part of what made him a good broadcast partner. Generosity helped, too. A while back, Jack Flaherty took a no-hitter into the late innings. It was Mike's inning to work. But Mike Claiborne had never called a no-hitter. Without fanfare and matter-of-factly, Shannon told Claiborne, "I've called no-hitters. Why don't you take this one?" The no-hitter slipped away in the seventh, but Mike Claiborne will remember that simple act of friendship long after the game's particulars are forgotten.

Claiborne and I were among the many broadcasting regulars at Shannon's restaurant near the ballpark. It was the perfect pregame or postgame baseball destination. The décor and the vast array of memorabilia were perfect. The menu was damn good, too. And after a night game at Busch, Mike was able to get just about anybody—superstars and legends included—to come over to be on his open-ended, postgame talk show, which pretty much began when he got there and ended when he decided it should.

Sitting around a large table beneath a very cool mural depicting Mike, Jack Buck, and other St. Louis sports figures in the Cardinals booth, Mike conducted freewheeling conversations filled with laughter and great baseball talk. "We're visiting with Don Zimmer…and, hey, look who just walked in: Harry Caray! Pull up a chair, Harry. Tomorrow night the Giants are in town, and Frank Robinson will join us."

It was like that all the time. Some of the best possible baseball atmosphere and conversation in the best baseball town took place there. Just one of the many aspects of Mike Shannon's baseball career and life that taken together added up to a one-of-a-kind public persona.

Now back to our lone reader in Tacoma or Bangor. That's the best I can do in explaining Mike Shannon. You sort of had to be there for all—or a good part—of it to really get it. Thankfully, the vast majority of you who have read to this point were there, at least as part of the audience, and you have your own recollections. Mike has his, too, so I'll let him take it from here.

—Bob Costas

Introduction

M y first exposure to Mike Shannon was as a college freshman Cardinals fan listening to the 50,000 red-hot watts of KMOX radio while I was in Quincy, Illinois, about 125 miles from St. Louis. Judging from what Harry Caray told me, young Mike, an outfielder then, was a raw-boned, former three-sport athlete who had some trouble hitting the curveball but also could hit a ball a long way and, likewise, throw it a long way from right field.

The 1964 season, which resulted in the Cardinals' first World Series title in 18 years, was one for the books as the Cardinals made up six-and-a-half games in less than two weeks down the stretch. It became a four-team pennant race, and KMOX, the Voice of St. Louis, would take us to other locales where big games were going on and cut into their radio feeds when the Cardinals' game was over—or if they weren't playing—whether it was Philadelphia, Cincinnati, Pittsburgh, San Francisco, or wherever.

Finally, with Bob Gibson pitching four innings of relief on one day's rest, the Cardinals won the pennant on the final day of the season. Mike Shannon, the hometown boy, homered in his first World Series game against the New York Yankees three days later, breaking a letter in the Budweiser sign on the scoreboard.

A couple of days later, I was painting my parents' bedroom and watching on television as Shannon was trying to save a game-ending home run by bracing himself on the low, three-foot wall in Yankee Stadium's right field, trying to snag a Mickey Mantle drive, which went off the face of the upper deck and almost out of Yankee Stadium. I wondered then, *What could he be thinking?* That question will be asked several times in this book, but the answer will come down to the given that there is always a method to Shannon's madness.

I was in the Army in 1968 when Shannon played in his final World Series and wasn't following the Cardinals as closely through the next three years, though I do remember the sadness associated with the kidney disease, which ultimately cut short his playing career.

But in 1971 I joined the *St. Louis Post-Dispatch* sports department, for which I still work. In 1972 Mike Shannon joined the Cardinals' broadcast team. In 1973 I covered my first Cardinals game, though I didn't take over the full-time beat until 1978.

When I encountered Mike for the first time, he was almost a larger-than-life figure. I could see he was tireless. He might catch 20 or 30 minutes of sleep on a plane. Sitting on the right side of the plane, he would keep his left hand in the air, holding the strap to the luggage compartment above his head, and that might be his sleep for the night. Traveling with the team on planes and buses then, I also soon figured out that Mike let nothing get in his way. He would sit in the seat behind the bus driver. Getting on the bus ahead of Mike one day, I put my heavy computer behind the driver and not really in Mike's way. I didn't think so, at least.

But when Mike took his seat and the bus was about to depart, he bellowed and kicked the bulky computer down the steps. I was sitting about three rows behind him and jumped up quickly, just in time before the computer rolled out the bus door and into New York City traffic, where it wouldn't have had much of a shelf life. And I wondered for the first time in 15 years, *What could he have been thinking?*

He didn't offer up much of an explanation, and we went our separate ways. But as the years went on and Mike had several different broadcasting partners from Jack Buck to Joe Buck to John Rooney—with a few in between—Mike and I gradually became friends. As the century changed from 20 to 21, he was still there covering the Cardinals, and so was I. I got to be a guest on the very popular *Live at Shannon's* radio show after weekend games, which was something of a coup for me. I had come to appreciate the fact that Mike had come a long way from not being very articulate on the air at first to being a real teacher of the game to the audience. I had no idea he knew so much about baseball and how it was played or should be played.

It eventually dawned on me that nobody had written the definitive Mike Shannon book.

I broached the topic with him about three years ago, and after some reflection, he decided that if he ever wanted to write a book, he wanted me to do it. A year or so passed without his mentioning it again until one day late in the lamentable 2020 season, Mike Claiborne, a broadcast partner of Mike's, said Mike wanted to see me. I went to the broadcast booth, and Mike said he wanted to do the book.

At that point, Mike had determined 2021 would be his 50th and final season in the booth. But our interviewing was delayed in large part because Mike was hit hard with COVID-19 just after the 2020 season ended. Finally, we began the process in spring training of 2021 in Jupiter, Florida, and some nine months later, we had our finished product. My hope is that Mike—with a little help from me and friends like Bob Costas, Tim McCarver, Joe Buck, Tony La Russa, Bob Uecker, Bud Selig, John Rooney, Dal Maxvill, and Vin Scully—brought you up close and personal to help understand, *What could he have been thinking?*

—Rick Hummel

CHAPTER 1

A Second Rally from Death

In my 50 years behind the microphone, I've had a few words I had trouble pronouncing but I had no trouble with these three: idiopathic membranous glomerulonephrhtis. It's a defect of the filtering function of the kidney. Idiopathic means it's a disease or condition, which arises spontaneously or for which the cause is unknown. I asked the doctors, "How do you get that? I didn't want to embarrass my family." They told me you can get it from a bee sting.

This kidney ailment forced a halt to my playing career in 1970, and in the end, it opened the doors to my broadcasting career. They said I could have died from this disease, and 50 years later, I almost died from the latest dangerous illness to hit our society—COVID-19.

But let's go back to the first disease—the kidney disease. I never really felt bad with it. They had found it during a test in spring training. We thought it was just a routine physical.

What happened was that the nephritis had attacked the filters in my kidneys and caused toxins to remain in my system. So I wasn't slowing down. I had an illness and I really didn't know how long I had been playing with it.

The good thing—if there is a good thing—is that when I got nephritis, the world's foremost kidney specialist in the world, Rex Jamison, happened to be in St. Louis at the time at Jewish Hospital. I was just lucky to have him when I got sent back to St. Louis from Florida, where we were training in St. Petersburg. Our team doctor, Stan London, was in his first year with the club. Character is what I go by a lot. And he showed me character, so I made him what I called my "general manager." He said this was a little out of his expertise and he was going to recommend a kidney guy, and that was Jamison. But I told him I still wanted him as my general manager. He did a helluva job. But at one point, London told my wife, "He's going down, down, down. He's not getting better."

I said, "What does the kidney specialist say?"

He said, "Give it two more weeks. Give it two more weeks. Give it two more weeks." And I kept doing that because I have a lot of respect for him.

I turned around the very next day and went the other way. The medicine they gave me worked. Basically, it was either going to work or it was *banzai* for me.

I'd be sleeping 19 or 20 hours a day. I'd eat a pound of bacon every day because it was protein and a half of loaf of bread because I was just so hungry. I'd wake up in a pool of water because it was so hot, but I'd be cold when I went to bed. That lasted as long as I could remember until I could start getting well. Jamison had patience and he'd do my blood test every day. He said, "You weigh 290 pounds. You've turned the page."

I looked at him and I said, "What?"

He said, "Trust me," and I did.

They took a piece of nephron out of my kidney and they had a piece of equipment over at Scott Air Force Base in Belleville, Illinois, and they sent that over to them. I got to watch it on the television monitor—you could see the needle going in when they took that piece of nephron out.

What happens with that disease is that it affects kids 12 and under, and it skips until about 30. I was 30, so I was the classic case. I was also the guinea pig because I was an athlete in perfect condition and I got the disease. The year before, in 1969, I was slowing down and I couldn't figure it out. So I decided that I had to train better and I already had adjusted my diet and training regimen before the physical. I used to drink a lot of coffee. But when I started living right and eating right, my boiler was still killing me. My wife, Judy, said that it was the coffee I was drinking. I told her that was a bunch of crap, but the next day, she made me decaf coffee, and it cleared up just like that. So I've been drinking decaf ever since I was 30. More than 50 years, I've done that. Boy, that goes fast.

On the down side, I was taking steroids, huge doses of prednisone, which they generally give you for heart problems. But I took more prednisone than anyone alive took for a prolonged period of time. They'd give a guy about 200 milligrams a week for a heart problem. I took 120 milligrams a day for about 180 days. Nobody had ever done that. I went from playing baseball every day to weighing 250 to 290 pounds. I was so fat I couldn't tie my shoes. The great Jack Buck once said that when he visited me that my head looked like a basketball.

Judy was at the hospital every day keeping everyone's spirits up, and eventually the kidney responded where I could play again—for a while. I came back in the middle of May, but I just wasn't the same. I had put on so much weight. And I still wasn't ready. I started playing on May 14 and lasted about three months. I didn't hit a home run and I had only 11 extra-base hits as I hit a not very productive .213. Only seven times did I have more than one hit in a game. I probably should have waited another year. But, again, I'm not a very patient guy.

I had five kids and I had to make some big decisions.

The biggest one was on August 12, 1970, at Busch Stadium, and I never played again. Of course, my last game I played 14 innings with my condition. But Bob Gibson pitched all 14 innings—we beat the San Diego Padres 5–4—and he never complained. I didn't even realize it was 14 innings. How in the hell are you going to come out of the game when that SOB pitches all 14 innings? It was different back then. If you started the game, you played the whole game. If it was 20 innings, it was 20 innings.

I had two hits, but I flied out in my last at-bat. But I had tried to take out a guy (second baseman Dave Campbell) on a double play in the second inning and I knew that Dr. London was coming for me after the game. I just knew he was going to say, "That's it." If I would have got kicked in the kidney, that would be all. I guess Dr. London didn't want to be responsible for that and I can't say that I blame him.

I was only 31 years old at the time when I stopped playing. But I was still taking that medicine, and they told me it would take like two years to come off it. The recovery went slowly but surely. And it's water-retaining, so my weight would have been a big problem. If I could have kept playing, I could have saved them from signing other guys because I could catch, so they really had to carry only two catchers. And I could play third base and the outfield. They had Ted Simmons, who caught every day.

I was disappointed to end my playing days, but I was really so happy to be alive. It wasn't a matter of a career. It was a matter of living and dying so I was happy about living. And I wasn't happy about the dying part. I made some promises to God. I needed to be there for my family if he would let me go on. I had five kids, and they were all young. He must have said, "I'll let you go on. But I've got some other stuff coming for you later on. You want more? I'll give you more."

But it is what it is. If you're going to step on your bottom lip, you're just wasting time.

I wanted to stay in the game at this point. Bing Devine, the general manager, wanted me to manage in Triple A at Tulsa, Oklahoma. Devine had been our general manager before he got fired late in our World Series year of 1964, went to the New York Mets to help build them into a power, and then had come back to the Cardinals.

I think Devine really wanted me to manage the Cardinals in the long run, but I didn't want to be away from my family and put in as much time as managers have to put in. That was the big reason. Judy had devoted all her time to taking care of me—she died of brain cancer in 2007 after we were married for 48 years—and I'm lucky now I've got a second wife, Lori, who does the same thing. She takes great care of me.

Anyhow, it was a tough decision going from playing every day to zero. I didn't know what to do. And then Devine came to me and asked about the Triple A job. I had to turn him down, and it was hard to get a job back then, I'll tell you. I went into sales for a year. I was assistant director of promotions and sales and I think they were just looking for a spot to put me. I enjoyed working in the Cardinals' front office, but I didn't really like the 9 to 5 part of it. If I could get my work done sooner than 9 to 5, I would like to be gone. But I would stay as long as I needed to get my work done.

Then the radio job came up, which was really fortunate. Harry Caray, the voice of the Cardinals for so many years, had left after the 1969 season, and a spot was open. They were trying to hire Don Drysdale, the former pitching great who was broadcasting for the Los Angeles Dodgers and doing national work, too, but Drysdale kept asking for more and more. Every time they presented him with a contract, he'd ask for something else.

At the time, I was just looking for a job, but I had learned a lot in the front office in that sales job, though I had no idea what I was getting into. And I had no idea the broadcast job was going to last 50 years and all the stuff that goes along with it. I had no idea at all. I was just happy to have a job period, especially with five kids. (We had another one later named Erin.)

But I've really enjoyed it. Sometimes you can't see the forest for the trees because I didn't realize what a tremendous position it was at the time. Being the voice of the Cardinals and all that means…I've kind of grown into that situation. I don't consider myself that good or that important—let's put it that way. But when you ask the people in the listening audience what they think about it, it's different. It is important. I've become important because of them. I didn't realize that until four or five years ago when they said, "Don't retire."

Then I realized how important the job was. And it is. There were a lot of people disappointed that 2021 was going to be my last year. Well, damn, I was going to be 82 years old. You can't work forever—except if you're Bob Uecker, the great Milwaukee broadcaster who was a catcher for us in the 1960s and a teammate of mine. He said he was going to die up there in the booth. And he might. He's 88 and still going strong.

But while this job is tough, it is not harder than playing. Baseball was hard for me. Football was easy, but baseball was hard. In football I'd come up to the line as a quarterback and know what everybody was going to do on the defensive side of the ball before they knew what they were going to do. It just came easy to me, you know. And I might have been a really good quarterback not only in college, but also the pros.

What wasn't so easy was COVID. I got COVID at the end of October in 2020 and I was in the hospital for 15 days. At first, they tried one medicine for five days, and I was going down the tubes. And then they gave me the stuff they gave President Trump, and that turned the trick. Regeneron monoclonal antibody cocktail was what it was.

But the first five days, I didn't recognize anything. I was completely out of it. And then the last five days, I just wanted to get the hell out of the hospital. I told them I would leave in the nude if I had to. I said, "I'm leaving tomorrow. I don't care what you say."

I found out I had it because my energy level was way down. Usually, it's way up compared to the average man. It just sapped my energy. And I'm not anything without energy as I think I displayed for most of the first 80 years of my life. Somebody asked me if this was scarier than nephritis. My answer is that it was just another challenge. It is what it is. You just face it. The coronavirus was not going to stop me from getting my 50th year in in the booth. It was just gonna take a long time to get better.

But I wasn't scared in the hospital because for the first few days I didn't know what the hell was going on. When I started to get better, I told the doctors, "I don't give a damn what you say." I'm not a very good patient. Never have been. At one point, I even yanked the PICC (central catheter) line out of my arm. I just think I'm Superman.

It was really bad. But it wasn't like I wasn't used to hospitals. I had a valve replacement in my heart a few years before that. If they hadn't given me that medicine that President Trump had…well, I'd have a different perspective about things now.

I did some things wrong because I'm such a hard-headed guy. I didn't do the rehab and I went deer hunting when I shouldn't have and I injured myself, and Lori got very upset with me. I can see the value of the rehab and I've got to stick with it. I went away from it the first time, but I won't this time. After all, I've got plans. Now that I've finished this broadcasting gig, I'll still have a job within the organization. And then, on June 6, 2044, the 100th anniversary of D-Day, I want to go back to Omaha Beach in France where Lori— she's a travel agent—and I visited a few years back.

I want to see a time capsule buried there on June 6, 1969, by the newsmen who covered the Allied Forces landing under Dwight D. Eisenhower on Normandy and then storming the beach as one of the most dramatic parts of World War II. I'll be 104, almost 105 on the 100th anniversary. I told my wife, "I'll push you up the hill. But…you'll have to walk back."

You talk about history. What those guys had to do—they had to go so far to get onto those beaches. That day changed the course of the world.

I look at life this way: there's a lot of good things that have happened. And a lot of bad things. But we've conquered them. Anything that happens, it's just another challenge. They say you get nine lives. I used one of them up when I had nephritis, but how many did I use while I was drinking and stuff? That's what worries me now. How many do I have left? I hope I have two or three because I'm planning on using them up when it's over.

I was 30 years old when I had nephritis, but I was in such good health and a young man at that point. But this last one, COVID, was much worse. I know I almost died. And Lori had it, too.

Speaking of hospitals, I was in one for so long when I had the kidney disease that I knew all the back stairways to get anywhere. One night our great righthander, Gibson, was in the hospital. He had wrenched his knee in New York in a play at first base and was still having trouble so they put him in the hospital overnight. So I decided I would go up the back steps and leave him a bottle of a champagne in his room.

The next day I go see him through the regular channels and he said, "I had the damnedest dream last night. I dreamed you were here." I never told him any different. I didn't want to spoil his good dream. So you can have some fun in hospitals, though it doesn't happen very often.

LORI SHANNON

Mike went to the hospital on October 20, 2020. Within four hours he went from normal Mike Shannon, to "I can't breathe Mike Shannon," to hanging his head out the window while I'm driving 80 miles an hour out to St. Luke's Hospital in St. Louis County on Highway 40.

We got there and he took seven liters, 15 liters, then 30 liters of oxygen. We had to go to the intensive care unit, and then within the next hour, he was so agitated and so upset because he was down for the count. He was in a medical coma because they had to put him out. COVID-19 had taken over so quickly. He was in that unit for nine days, and then they moved him to the Critical Care Unit for six days. We kept it quiet for a while because that's the way Mike wanted it. Not even the rest of the family and certainly no media because that would have created extra attention.

Soon enough, everybody found out. But that was a scare for everyone. I know I was scared. The first five days in the hospital, when he wasn't responding to any of the medicines, they told me to get our life in order. They told me he wasn't going to make it. So I called his oldest son, Mike Jr., and said, "I've got to tell you something about your dad."

I wound up getting COVID, too, but not as bad—I was asymptomatic. I would call the hospital every two hours. One day they called and they said Mike wasn't responding to a certain drug and, in fact, was doing worse, so they told me they wanted to give him regeneron, which was the drug President Trump took. The day before, they said they couldn't get it, but they said they had found some. So I drove out there—I still had to stay in my car—and signed a packet of papers so they could give him the regeneron.

There was no time to read it, so I signed everything and handed it back to them. This was about 2:30 in the afternoon. They called me back at 4:30 and said they just had given him the first dose. Within four hours, they said that he was starting to change, which was good. But he was just laying there. He didn't want to be ventilated, but they wanted him to be. They also wanted to tie him down to the bed because he was so aggravated. I said, "If you touch him, if you tie him down, if you vent him, this will be called St. Lori's Hospital rather than St. Luke's. Do not touch my husband."

The doctor was a young resident and he was really tall so I had to reach up to get in his face. I'm not sure he and the nurses got along super well. The nurses there were unbelievable, by the way. The next morning, when I called, they said Mike was responding, and he just kept getting better and better and better. Finally, he got to leave the hospital on November 5. That was the first time I had seen him since he had gone to the hospital.

When this all started and you see it on TV from New York with all these people and the big graves and stuff, it was overwhelming, and I had to shut the TV off. I got to where I didn't even watch the news anymore. Everybody was watching it on TV and saying, "Oh, my gosh, I can't believe this is happening." That's one thing, but when you live it, it's a whole other level. It was very scary, unbelievably scary. But I have nothing bad to say about St. Luke's. They were incredible. I called every two hours for 14 days and talked to the nurses.

How hard did he fight this? This is a guy who pulled out his own catheter line, which went to his heart. He was just so confused and angry... and on so many drugs. And, yes, going deer hunting was a bad idea, an awful idea. But (blank) happens. He thinks he's Superman. A couple of years ago, I even bought him a Superman T-shirt for Christmas.

CHAPTER 2

Stan the Man

I had a Stan Musial glove as a kid, and "Mr. Musial" was a cool dad. I probably paid more attention to him as a ballplayer than his son, Dick, did. But Stan Musial was a shrewd adviser, too. I had a scholarship to play quarterback at the University of Missouri, but I was also was a top baseball prospect. But in 1957 baseball still had the rule that if a "bonus baby" got $4,000 or more, he had to stay in the big leagues and couldn't play in the minors that year or the next. I was likely to get much more than that, but Stan advised me not to sign and to go to Mizzou because he said that Major League Baseball was going to get rid of that rule soon, and Stan ended up being correct. USC had tried to recruit me, too, to play football, but USC was so far away I thought it was in Japan. However, my son, Tim, signed there 20 years later to play football.

I left Missouri after one year and signed with the St. Louis Cardinals in 1958 for almost $100,000 but was allowed to start my career in the minors, where I belonged.

Sandy Koufax got caught under the rule and had to stay in the big leagues for two years with the Dodgers. It really hurt him. He should have been pitching somewhere and he might have turned out to be even greater than he turned out to be. I guess it didn't hurt him that much, considering how good he was. He is in the Hall of Fame after all.

This was well before the draft, which began in 1965, and the rule had been implemented to prevent the wealthiest teams like the New York Yankees and Dodgers from signing all the best players and then stashing them in the minors. There would be no minors for these players for at least two years, and some players, like Al Kaline and Koufax, never saw the minors at all. But the bonus babies virtually saw no big league time at all for two years. The Philadelphia Phillies had a pitcher, Tom Qualters, who pitched exactly one-third of an inning in 1953 and not at all in 1954. Then he was finally able to go to the minors. He didn't come back until 1957 and never won a game in the majors.

There's no question that the money pushed me into baseball. But the Cardinals had time to wait on me. They had both Gary Kolb and me to replace Musial when he retired. It wound up that they traded for Lou Brock from the Chicago Cubs. After the 1963 season, Musial's last, I stayed around, but Kolb went on to the Milwaukee Braves, the New York Mets, and the Pittsburgh Pirates. Like me, he had been a big high school multi-sport star, having been on a second-place team in the state basketball championship while he was at Rock Falls, Illinois.

At Christian Brothers College, Dick Musial was the star halfback with me as the elite quarterback. We were playing our archrivals, St. Louis U. High, and the defense was really after him because he was Stan Musial's son. Dick ran for a long touchdown. But the officials called it back because somebody was holding. So I called the same play, and Dick ran for another touchdown and I came to the line and said to the defense, "Hey, you want any more of that Musial kid?'"

We pretty much had our way with the teams we played because we had a terrific offensive line and some really good skill players.

I was a really good basketball player, but I was only a 6'2" center. I got scholarship offers for both, though many more for football. I could have gone about anywhere in the country for football. But, of course, I did like playing baseball, too, and also basketball, even though there was no professional future—and not much of a college one—for a 6'2" center.

One time we were playing St. Louis U. High, and it had a 7'0", 290-pound center named Bob "Bevo" Nordmann, who went on to star at St. Louis University. Our coach, the great D.C. Wilcutt, said, "I want you to foul him out."

But I took a beating. I told Wilcutt, "After about the fourth foul, I think you're going to have to get a new center." Bevo had figured out Wilcutt's strategy—and mine, too, I guess. On the third foul, Nordmann knocked me so far into the seats it took me a ticket to get back.

I will always treasure my days at CBC and will always treasure having the baseball field named after me. I always had been a star athlete as young player. You always know when you're pretty good. I was 11 years old, playing with guys much older in organized leagues. When I was 11, there really wasn't any place organized to play—just pick-up games. But they had this league where the maximum age was 15. Somebody asked me to join—I had been playing with those guys anyway—and you could be younger, even as young as I was, and my first official position was center field.

When I first got to the Cardinals and joined Stan Musial, I graduated to calling Musial "Stan the Man." He memorably noted, "When your teammates are your kids' playmates, it's time to retire."

He was admired by players and front-office people from other teams beside his own. Horace Stoneham, who owned the San Francisco Giants, was a good friend of his, and Stoneham was an alcoholic evidently. Musial told Johnny Keane, our manager, that he didn't want to play in a Thursday day game late in September of 1962 because he was going out with Stoneham the night before and going to be up all night. Musial came in the following morning, and his name was in the lineup because a bunch of guys had gotten sick. Musial didn't say a word to Keane, though he surely hadn't counted on playing. Stoneham was sitting up there in the press box thinking, *After all these years, this is finally the day we get this guy out.* But Musial went 5-for-5 off three different pitchers.

He got his first three hits off Billy "Digger" O'Dell, who was about as tough a left-hander as there was. He then singled off Jim Duffalo in the seventh and again off relief specialist Stu Miller, his old Cardinals teammate, in the ninth inning. On the last at-bat, it was a 3–2 fastball sinking inside, and Musial fouled it straight back. Then, he fouled a slider away. And then he got a base hit to left field. That's how great Musial was. He didn't even expect to play but got five hits while being hungover. And we won the game 7–4, which could have put a crimp in the Giants' hopes of winning the National League pennant. But they managed a tie for the title on the final day of the regular season and then beat the Dodgers in a three-game playoff.

Guys like Musial and Ted Williams just slowed the game down, where a human being like myself had to fight for everything. You learn the game that way, I'll tell you that. I would go in for Musial late in the game if the other team had a left-hander and Kolb, who was a left-handed hitter, would go in for Musial on defense if the other team had a right-hander pitching.

So, it took two young guys to replace one old guy. However, that one old guy was pretty good.

I just happened to stay longer in the game than Kolb. I got on better teams than he got on. But I also deserved it. I was a better athlete. I'm still the only guy who won the best high school basketball player and best football player awards in the state of Missouri in the same year. And I'm very proud of that. Yet I went into pro baseball.

Musial didn't make any mistakes on or off the field. I remember one time talking to him about hitting. He said there was a little imaginary cone about 10 feet out in front of the plate. Once that ball got inside that cone, then he decided what he was going to do with it, meaning whether he wanted to swing and where he wanted to hit it. I told him I didn't see that cone. I'm still waiting to see it. I knew right then and there I was way out of my league. Guys like him actually slowed the ball down with their eyesight. They would isolate the ball.

Both he and Williams had bad years when they were about 40 and bounced back to have great seasons the next year. Musial batted .330 when he was 41 years old after he hit .288 when he was 40, and Williams hit .254 at 40 and then batted .316 when he was 41. There was no way I was going to be playing at age 40 or 41. I didn't make it past 31.

I'd go look at Musial's bat at about the middle of July, and it only had marks on the sweet spot. Mine were up and down on both sides, and his all were on the sweet spot. That was the most amazing thing to me—how he could hit the ball there every time. He once told me that it was not productive to hit the ball up the middle. Asked to expand on that, Musial said, "Well, that's where the best players are playing, and it's the biggest part of the ballpark."

They don't make many Stan Musials anymore. They haven't made any. Thank God, somewhere along the line, somebody must have said, "Don't mess with that screwy stance he has."

I know our hitting coach, Harry Walker, was always standing next to Musial. I think he had his belt hooked to him. I said, "Hey, Harry, how about us .250 hitters? We could use some help here." He must have thought I was a poisonous snake the way he backed away from me and got closer to Musial. Walker wasn't so dumb, as it turned out.

And what was really amazing about Musial was that he got the same amount of hits on the road as he did at home—1,815. He got two hits in his final game in 1963 and then came out of the game with 1,815 hits at home to match his road total. Musial never seemed to make a mistake, and that includes the year when he was general manager in 1967. When I found out he was going to be the GM, I called Dal Maxvill (the Cardinals' shortstop) and said, "Maxie, we'll probably win the pennant by 10 games. Stan's never wrong."

I was wrong. We won by 10½ games.

We went without 25 players for almost a month because Musial said we didn't need that many. So we played with 24.

Not many things bothered Musial, but he was scared of hospitals. One time, Musial was planning to get his knees operated on. His good friend, Yogi Berra, who was with the Yankees but grew up in St. Louis, had just gone through it, so Musial called the catching great, who said, "Ah, there's nothing to it." So Musial got the operation for his knees, and after that they were just killing him, and eventually he called Berra back and said, "Why, you SOB."

The best story is I can tell you about Musial also took place in 1962, a few days ahead of his five-hit game. I had just been called up from the minors, and we're playing a Monday afternoon game in Wrigley Field in Chicago in September, and there's no one there. The attendance was 1,600. Musial was a little sore and he wasn't playing that day so I was playing left field. And this guy and his son were sitting in the box seats, and the father was giving me the business. And I could hear it because nobody was there. He says, "Shannon, where's Musial?"

I said, "He's not playing today."

He said, "You mean I drove 750 miles from Kansas to see Stan Musial play his last game in Chicago and I have to watch you play left field?"

I felt so sorry for him. I can imagine him driving all that way and telling his kid, "You're going to see the best." And he had to watch me play left field. Not the best.

I had been all excited about it. Keane had come to me and said, "You're playing left field today. Stan's too tired." I thought, *great.* Then this guy yelling at me goes on for a while, and finally about the third inning, I come into the dugout along the first-base side and climb the stairs leading up to the visiting clubhouse at Wrigley.

Musial's taking a nap on the training table while getting worked on, and I tell him this fan, who's brought his son from miles and miles away, is all over me. So I asked him to sign a ball for me that I could take back down to the fan. Musial signed one. I put it in my pocket, and the next inning, I tossed it to the guy, and from then on, the rest of the game it's: "Attaboy, Shannon. You're the man."

I didn't give him much else, though. I went nothing for four. But Stan was really the man.

If you didn't know him, you wanted to meet him.

When I had the restaurant in downtown St. Louis, Tony La Russa, who was managing the Cardinals then, said,

"Hey, a friend of mine wants to meet Stan Musial. Can you introduce him?"

I said, "Sure."

It was Jerry Reinsdorf, the Chicago White Sox owner, and I said it would be my pleasure. So I set up a dinner at the restaurant with Reinsdorf and La Russa and I think Musial brought his wife, Lil, and Red Schoendienst, another Hall of Famer, with him.

It had a big impact on Reinsdorf to meet Musial. The impact Musial had on people was phenomenal. I could tell you stories about him forever. He was as trusted a man as you would ever find. If he told you he would be somewhere at 3:00, he would be there at 3:00 sharp. Up until a month before he died at age 92 in January of 2013, Musial regularly would show up at the offices of Stan the Man Inc. on Des Peres Road in St. Louis County to autograph balls, pictures, caps, bats, jerseys, or whatever other memorabilia was placed in front of him.

For most of the nearly quarter-century existence of Stan the Man Inc., Musial was like clockwork—much the way he treated hitting a baseball for 22 seasons from 1941 to 1963. Every weekday morning from 10:30 to 11:30, Musial would be at the company offices signing. Then it was off to lunch with a restaurant rotation, including Schneithorst's, the Missouri Athletic Club West, and Busch's Grove, the latter of which would mean that it was Tuesday, and it was time for ham and eggs, and good friend Jack Buck would be a lunch companion.

I'd heard Musial did not like to be late for his signing sessions nor did he suffer being late for anything else on his docket. He loved his routine. Hell hath no fury if you were late for anything. He would even command whoever was driving him to whip through a parking lot so he could make his lunch reservation on time.

For nearly two years after his death, his signed memorabilia continued to be of considerable interest to collectors. People were allowed to come into Stan the Man Inc's offices and just talk. Musial was so affable that he wouldn't turn anybody down, his agent, Dick Zitzmann said. Musial loved it; he really did. He would take pictures with people. He was almost too good. But Musial did have his own method of speeding along the process. When he saw people fishing in their pockets for an item for him to sign, he would pull out signed postcards from his pocket. He always had those with him. "I had heard from talking to other people that as a young man Stan was fairly shy," Zitzman said. "But he really learned how to be outgoing and to be somebody for the people. I guess that's why everybody in our town loved him."

DICK MUSIAL

At the time when we played football in high school at Christian Brothers College, Mike was a much better football player than baseball player. He was a superb football player. He was the quarterback and he would change the play at the line of scrimmage, and our coach would scream, "Why did you change the play?"

And Mike would say, "Why do you care? We just got 20 yards."

That was typical Michael. He was not a great cadet in that military atmosphere, but he was a great athlete.

We went unbeaten in his senior season and my junior season, and the big game was always against St. Louis U. High. We had a great quarterback in Mike and a terrific offensive line that averaged about 200 pounds a man, which in the 1950s was huge for a high school offensive line. And I was a fast halfback then. Mike would call a play that I knew the coach didn't call and he would say, "Don't worry about it. Just go to the right, and I'll get it to you."

And it worked. It was like sandlot football in a lot of ways and it was a lot of fun in many ways. That line made it so much easier for Mike and that halfback.

Dad, of course, went to every game during the football season and he really enjoyed it. And, you know, my dad and Michael had a great relationship, and Dad very much wanted him to succeed. He was helping Mike get into Mizzou and giving him direction. He recognized Mike's ability. Dan Devine had taken over Mizzou's football program in Mike's freshman year, and Mike was looking good as the quarterback for the next year's varsity team. But the St. Louis Cardinals were his love. After his freshman year, he signed with the

Cardinals and got the money. That became important because he was getting married, and he and his wife, Judy, were starting a family. She was a great gal.

But I'm absolutely convinced that if Mike had stayed with football, he would have been a star in college and in the pros, too. In high school Mike could probably throw that ball 50 yards. Yeah, I think he had a good shot at pro football, I really do. But I'm glad he went to baseball.

Without Mike at third base in the 1967 season—he really had to work at that position when the Cardinals won the World Series that year—the Cardinals might not have won it all. And Mike was a big-time player. He homered in each of the three World Series he played in—once off Whitey Ford of the New York Yankees and once off Mickey Lolich of the Detroit Tigers.

Dad finally had retired by then and really enjoyed that line of his when he said it was time to retire when your teammates used to be your son's playmates. You know Dad played so long. Normally, when they're 30, 32 years old, they're gone. Dad played until he was almost 42 years old. He was a tremendous athlete and he had a high threshold for pain. I don't really know how he did it.

Mike was in line as one of the guys to replace Dad, but Dad kept on playing. Finally, Mike got his chance. He had a good career and without a doubt has done a great job at announcing and improved himself tremendously over the last 50 years. I've lived in Florida for many years now and I would always enjoy our visits to the booth in Jupiter, Florida, for spring training with the Cardinals. How could you not want to be there? Mike Shannon was there and so were the Cardinals.

CHAPTER 3

Baseball or Football

As a kid I used to throw the tennis ball off the front steps and pretend that Harry Caray was announcing the game, telling people I was making all those great, diving plays. But my real love was football. When I was a quarterback and I came up to the line, I already knew what was going to happen on defense. It was just natural. That scared some people, but that's the way I was.

Coach Frank Broyles put a great freshman team together at Missouri—you couldn't play on the varsity then because of NCAA rules—and *Sport* magazine called it the greatest freshman team ever assembled. But before the next spring was over, Broyles had taken the Arkansas job and he called me in right before he left. Evidently, the Arkansas people had talked to Broyles and said he couldn't take me with him. I can imagine the University of Missouri had said to Broyles: "You can go to Arkansas, but you're not taking any players." And he was a man of his word. He never asked me to follow him.

I was a Split-T quarterback, and he was a Split-T coach. Dan Devine became Missouri's coach and he was the same type of coach as Broyles. We had the spring game between the varsity and the freshmen in 1958. And we were better than the varsity. We should have beaten them. In fact, we had them beat until we lost it late. We had five high school All-Americans in the backfield. And we had another guy who was the best player of all, but he just couldn't read or write.

Before the game—it was about the second week of spring practice—Devine was calling the plays for the freshmen in the huddle. It was second and 1, and I changed the play. He almost swallowed his tongue. It was second and 1, and I had three chances to score the touchdown. The play worked. Two weeks later, I changed another play. He asked me why I changed the play on second and 1, and I said, "If you can't make it on third and 1, you've got a crappy team."

That's what I told him, and we didn't have a crappy team. But Devine was student-body left, student-body right in his philosophy.

I told Danny LaRose, who was a 6'7" All-American from Crystal City, Missouri, and had a defensive back, who was 5'6", trying to defend him, "Just run out in front of him and don't drop the damn thing." I wanted to impress Devine. LaRose caught the ball. I don't know how impressed

Devine was. LaRose, who finished eighth in the Heisman Trophy voting in his senior season of 1960, wound up being a defensive tackle in the pros for six years. The next time I sent Mel West downfield. He was a speedy, 5'9" guy from Jefferson City who ended up running kicks back for the New York Titans in the AFL. "I'll find you," I said. "Don't stop until the whistle blows."

Broyles later called me and told me I was going to start for him in 1958 at Mizzou if I had stayed because I would have been able to work out any mistakes I was making in the spring game that year. In 1960, the year I would have been a senior along with those other All-Americans, that Missouri team was so good. It went 11–0 and won the Orange Bowl. The Tigers could have ended up being national champions, but Kansas ran a 10-man line at them from the opening kickoff. It turns out that Kansas used an ineligible player, running back Bert Coan, who scored two touchdowns. Missouri later got a forfeit win but not the national title. I'd have beaten Kansas 100–0 if they'd run a 10-man line at me from the opening kickoff. I would have called time the first play of the game. Then I would have had gone over to face Devine, and he would have said, "Why'd you call timeout?"

I would have said, "Do you see what I see? Ten men on the line."

I would've had those two scatbacks—West and Norris Stevenson—for receivers. But I wasn't there, and Missouri didn't have a quarterback who passed much. Devine didn't call the pass much either, and Kansas stuffed the Tigers. If I had stayed at Mizzou, would I have been the Heisman winner? That's not for me to say, but Broyles said it. Missouri could have been national champions, and everything just fit. That would have been right place, right time. But what I couldn't understand was why they never went out and recruited a quarterback. They had Phil Snowden as their No. 1 guy, but he had a chronic arm problem.

In high school I also had been the St. Louis area's Player of the Year in basketball. I stayed back under the basket and then I'd run out and say, "Give me the ball."

I was a center, but I was a driving center, which was unheard of. We played this one team, and I drove around their center a couple of times for easy baskets. So, their coach called timeout and said, "We've got to lay off this guy."

The next time, I popped out from under the basket, and their center just stayed under the basket and waved his arms and yelled at me, trying to distract me. So I just shot the ball from the free-throw line. I played freshman ball at Missouri, but I don't know how effective I was as a 6'2" center.

When I was a senior in high school, we had this big 6'10" sophomore kid named Gary Garrison, who went on to play at St. Louis University. Our coach, D.C. Wilcutt, said to me, "You've got to push this kid around in practice."

So I pushed him around all right. But he got wind of that, and he said, "This is bull," and he started pushing back.

So I went to Wilcutt and said, "We need to call him off."

When I was in high school, all I tried to do was get passing grades. It wasn't until my senior year that the teachers said, "You'd better make the honor roll so you'll be an honor student." I made the honor roll because I could do what I needed to do—basically. But the only reason I went to school was so I could play ball honestly. I got all Cs until I learned I had to make the honor roll and I made the B honor roll.

But my big sports were football and baseball. I don't mind telling you that baseball was much harder for me. But it was the right place to go. It was like the fork in the road. You've got to take one or another. If I hadn't signed for baseball, I was going to transfer and go to USC to play football. I only had all Cs for my grades at Missouri, and normally you couldn't transfer unless you had As and Bs, but USC would have worked something out. Schools did that—still do—for a good athlete.

I'll never forget this. Twenty years later my son, Tim, was playing for USC in the Rose Bowl in Pasadena, California, and Broyles was doing the color commentary for ABC television. And we happened to be coming into the stadium at the same time. When he was recruiting me, he was a teetotaler. But when you came in to see my dad, you got a Budweiser handed to you. When he was at our house, Broyles looked at a tree we had and poured his beer into that. Twenty years later, he said to me at the stadium, "Is that tree still alive?"

It was artificial. So I told Broyles, "As far as I'm concerned, it still is. The Budweiser didn't hurt it."

I didn't go to USC and I took the money to sign with the St. Louis Cardinals. My first stop was Class D Albany, Georgia, in June of 1958. John Momford was the general manager and he picked me up and drove me to the ballpark, where we were playing a doubleheader. He got me a uniform, and there was nobody in the clubhouse. It was all dark, and then he took me onto the field and introduced me to the manager, who was player/manager Mo Mozzali. "You're playing center field and hitting fourth," Mozzali said.

I got two hits in each game and I think I won both games with a hit, so he thought he had a phenom. About midnight Momford was walking out of the clubhouse and I said, "Hey, where do I sleep?"

He said, "Oh, yeah, where do you sleep?"

Bill Martin was a catcher from Belleville, Illinois, and he was staying with a guy named Bob Boyer, who was no relation to Kenny, Cletis, or any of the big league Boyers.

But he was leading the team in home runs and he was a hell of a player. Bill took me home, and there was a blonde laying on the couch, and all she had on was fingernail polish. Bill said, "There's Boyer's room. There's my room. There's the bathroom, and that [girl] belongs to Boyer."

I stayed on the other side of the wall. When I got up in the morning, she was gone, and we went down to have breakfast. They didn't have a restaurant, but they had a drug store, so that's where I ate. I ordered bacon and eggs, and the place had this white stuff on the plate, and it was called grits. I've been eating grits ever since. I had never seen it or heard of it before. But it was Albany, Georgia, and everybody ate grits.

I hit .322 that year. And then instead of going to Class C ball, I skipped C and went to Class B ball at Winston-Salem, North Carolina, where I batted .273 with 14 homers. Then I skipped Class A ball and went to Class Double A in Memphis in 1960, where I teamed with Tim McCarver for the first time. I was there all season and batted .263 with nine homers and 79 RBIs, the most I ever drove in for a season. I wound up playing in Double A and Triple A ball for Tulsa and Portland in 1961, hitting 14 home runs and driving in 56. The next year it was Triple A at both Seattle and Atlanta, where I made a move, batting .288 with 75 RBIs.

Finally, I got to the big leagues at the end of the 1962 season. Then, it was back to Triple A the next year and again back to the big leagues. It was natural progression. I did hit my first big league homer in 1963. I had gone in for Stan Musial on defense and homered off Chicago Cubs pitcher Dick Ellsworth.

In 1964 I played the first half of the season in Jacksonville, Florida, in Triple A, where I hit .278 and then I got back to the big leagues, where I stayed. But I had come close to quitting. I had made up mind that if I didn't make the big leagues by 1962, I was going to call it a career because I was still young enough I could have gone into another field. I put a date on the wall in 1962. The day before that, the Cardinals called me up to the big leagues. No one knew about that date on the wall except me.

What would have I done? I don't know. I would have done anything. I figured if I didn't make it to the big leagues by that time, it wasn't going to happen. I never told anybody about it in the organization. But it just so happened they called me up the day before. I always had an interest in criminal law. I'd have retired for sure well before now if I had gone into that field, but 50 years later after I started broadcasting, I was doing the same damn thing and loving it. I was at the right time at the right place. The Cardinals have been very good to me. But they got their money's worth. I don't think there's a complaint on either side.

I don't regret passing up football for baseball. At the time, it was the right decision to make. It had to do with money. I got almost $100,000. That pushed me into baseball. But the Cardinals had time to wait on me. They had both Gary Kolb and me to replace Musial when he retired. Kolb got to run for Musial on the day he got his final two hits—both off Jim Maloney, the big Cincinnati Reds righthander. Both of them went just out of the reach of a rookie second baseman on the Reds by the name of Pete Rose. And then Rose broke Musial's record for hits almost 20 years later in Philadelphia when Rose was playing with the Phillies.

Even after I was in the majors, though, the Atlanta Falcons called me and wanted me to play quarterback for them in 1966. One of their coaches was at USC when they tried to recruit me out of high school. I accidentally ran into him at the hotel in Atlanta where we both were staying, and he invited me to lunch. The Falcons had just started up as an expansion team. I hadn't played football in eight years, and that was my question them to them: *Why would you want me as a quarterback?* He said they would figure it out when I got there.

Maybe I would have gotten crushed, especially if I had played quarterback, because an expansion football team like the Falcons generally isn't strong on the offensive line. Maybe they would have put me at some other position. Who knows? But football always had been in my blood, and there was some interest on my part because I wasn't playing regularly and I was hitting .216 or something. I gave the coach a dollar figure that I needed to switch sports.

But I started playing more regularly for the Cardinals. I hit .395 in July—I was Player of the Month—and that's what pooh-poohed that. Then I knew where my future in athletics was going to be. I didn't know, of course, I would be playing in two more World Series, giving me three for my career before the decade was over.

TIM McCARVER

I've said many, many times that if it had not been for Mike Shannon going over to third base from the outfield, that whole thing in 1967–68 wouldn't have worked. He solved a major, major problem by doing that. An outfielder turning into an infielder…that's tough to do. It's a lot tougher than going the other way around. When you go the other way around—from the infield to the outfield—the ball is not on top of you all of a sudden. But Mike had the arm to take care of all that stuff. And it was a tremendous, tremendous thing for Mike to be able to do that for us in St. Louis.

I've known Mike for more than 60 years when we were both with the Memphis Chicks in Class Double A, and the ballpark burned down. We had some great teams then and we played hard. We were competitive, including being competitive with each other. We didn't like to be embarrassed among our teammates. That was very important to us. And so it was that Mike worked very, very hard at being a good third baseman, and he talked to a lot of different third basemen. Don Hoak of the Pittsburgh Pirates is one that comes to mind. Don told him to play shallow, and I remember Mike telling me that was so the bad hops didn't have a chance to develop, which I thought was pretty savvy. That makes sense.

We confided in one another kind of. But his primary go-to guy was Roger Maris, and Roger helped him a great deal. Bob Gibson helped, too, because he didn't allow too many balls to be hit to third base unless he needed a double play. When Bob was in a double-play situation, he would throw that sinking fastball that resulted in a one-hopper to third. It was a kind of a marvel for Mike to know that Bob could do that. But Bob would work down and in to weak, right-handed hitters. Bob could get that double play pretty handily, and a lot of them went Mike's way.

Except for Roger coming in for 1967 and 1968, we had pretty much the same position player lineup for those World Series teams. We won the first two, but the one that still bothers me—and all of us—was losing to the Detroit Tigers in 1968 after we were up three games to one. Take nothing from the Tigers. They had a really good team. For them to win one game, Game Seven, from Gibson was monumental.

Mike and I would hang out together, but we rarely went out to dinner together because Mike was a steak man, and I occasionally liked things other than a steak. And he liked to stay out later than I did. I had different hours since I was catching every day. But I wasn't any choirboy either.

After we were through playing, we went on to long careers in broadcasting but never worked together. Nobody ever asked. Would I have been different working with Shannon? I don't know. But there were an awful lot of players on our teams who went into broadcasting. That gives you an idea of how good we were at analyzing our play and how well we knew the game. Dick Groat broadcast basketball until he was 90. Bill White did the New York Yankees games. Bob worked for the network for a while. Nellie Briles did the Pirates' games for many years.

We were self-effacing and honest about our play. That's the one thing we're still very good at. We're honest. When I was with the New York Mets and even doing TV with the St. Louis Cardinals, I was being so honest that management would occasionally get concerned about me being too honest. I've always thought being too honest was the right way to go. And I was always honest to myself. You can't fool the people who are listening. I never tried to. That's one thing I'm very proud of. I'm sure Mike has taken the same approach. We were all honest in the way we spoke to each other. I can hear Dick saying, "That ball's got to be caught." He was talking about himself, but he'd talk about you, too.

If you played on that team, you were going to learn a lot about baseball. I missed Mike's party after he finished up his 50 years in the radio booth. I sent him some flowers because I couldn't be there. I said, "The legend continues, remarkable as your career has been."

And I meant every word of it. Some guys turn down the same road that other guys do and they do it their way. If anybody did it their way, Mike did.

CHAPTER 4

Hitting Home Runs in the World Series

Although I got a lot of money for signing with the St. Louis Cardinals, my road to the majors was not a smooth one. I got to St. Louis in September of 1962 and got my first hit, a single, in my second at-bat against Cincinnati Reds pitcher Bob Purkey. He won 23 games that year, so I felt pretty good about that. We had only two other hits in that game off Purkey. Stan Musial and Kenny Boyer both homered.

But in 1963, when I was supposed to be with the Atlanta team in Triple A, I missed the first half of the season to be with my wife, Judy, who was pregnant back in St. Louis with our fourth child and was bedridden and had a hard time taking care of our other three kids. I had to be with her. Finally, in July of that year after I had spent a brief time in Atlanta, which was still a Triple A franchise then, I was brought up to St. Louis for the rest of the season, though I didn't play much as we won 19 of 20 games late in the year and almost ran down the Los Angeles Dodgers for the

National League pennant. That was when play-by-play man Harry Caray coined that catchy phrase, "The Cardinals are coming. Tra-la, Tra-la."

Then the Dodgers were the ones who were coming. They swept us in a three-game series in St. Louis in late September with little-known Dick Nen, who was playing his first game in the majors, hitting a game-tying home run in the ninth inning. The Dodgers scored an unearned run in the 13th inning to complete the sweep with a 6–5 win in a game we had led 5–1 behind Bob Gibson. The Dodgers went on to the pennant and then swept the New York Yankees in four games in the World Series.

After starting the season with the Cardinals in 1964, I spent May through July in Jacksonville, Florida, and did okay with 11 home runs and 33 RBIs. Then I came to St. Louis to stay at the All-Star break. I became the starting right fielder not long after that. As we made our charge toward the pennant in September, I had one stretch when I hit five homers in seven games and I had another home run rained out in Cincinnati. We had a big three-game sweep of the Philadelphia Phillies in the last week of the season in St. Louis when the Phillies were in the midst of their 10-game losing streak, and I drove in three runs in the first game that series. We finally pulled off an incredible comeback—we had trailed the Phillies by six-and-a-half games with 13 to go—

by beating the New York Mets 11–5 on the final day of the season after the Mets had beaten us in the first two games of the series. The Mets lost 109 games that year.

On the final Saturday, there were still four teams in the hunt, but then the San Francisco Giants fell out by losing to the Chicago Cubs. There never had been a four-way tie—or even a three-way tie—for the pennant. And we only had 10 teams in the league.

Before games on the final Sunday, we were tied with the Reds for first place with the Phillies a game behind. There were all sorts of playoff plans in place for a three-team playoff or just a two-teamer with us and the Reds. But the Phillies righted themselves after we sent them to their 10th straight loss by winning their final two games of the year at Cincinnati, including thrashing the Reds 10–0 in the last game on Sunday. We could see that score developing, but we had to win, too, or there would be a three-way tie.

Gibson, who lost 1–0 to the Mets on Friday night, came out of the bullpen to pitch four innings of relief on one day's rest, and we came back from being down 3–2 in the fifth inning.

I had a run-scoring single early in that game against New York. But that was nothing compared to the next time we played a New York team. That was in the World Series.

I got to play in my first World Series in my hometown. I singled my first time up and then I hit a two-run, game-tying homer off the New York Yankees' Whitey Ford my third time up in the sixth inning. He hung a slider to me. He had missed with two sliders inside. I took both of them, and then he hung one. A few years before that, he would have thrown a fastball, but he didn't have a fastball anymore. I always had trouble staying back on the off-speed pitches. I've just been so lucky. I played in the World Series in my hometown and I hit a home run off of Ford. Man, I'm a dreamer, but even I can't dream that good.

That home run had to be on the first page of all the papers in the world because it broke the "U" in the Budweiser sign out in left field. John Kern, who was with the sign company, showed me the bill, which was for about $5,000 and was going to be my whole World Series check. I only made $4,000 during the season. But Gussie Busch, our owner, said in that gravelly voice of his, "That's all right, buddy. You can break the whole sign down." And Gussie paid for it.

Since every paper had that picture, I guess I can thank that cameraman. When those signs first came out, if you broke one of the tubes, the whole sign went out, and I, of course, broke the letter after B. That's still the sign you see on Highway 64-40 going west out of St. Louis. After the game

I remember telling reporters that I had hit a better one about 450 feet in Dublin. "Dublin, Ireland?" somebody asked.

"No, Dublin, Georgia," I said.

That was one of the places we played when I was with Albany my first season.

There's also a famous picture of me in right field jumping for a home run that Mickey Mantle hit off Barney Schultz to win Game Three of the World Series in Yankee Stadium. The ball nearly went out of the stadium, but it hit the façade way up at the top. They had a little three-foot wall in front of the fans there, and I jumped for the ball. It may have hit that façade and come down and I was going to catch that sucker. You can trick those umpires sometimes.

I came off the field, and our catcher, Tim McCarver, said, "Moon, what were you doing? That ball nearly went out of the stadium."

I said, "Big boy, you never know."

My nickname, "Moon," is short for "Moon Man." I went over to Gibson one time at the mound. I was trying to distract him and I looked up at the sky and said, "There's going to be a guy that's going to walk on that moon one of these days."

So he started calling me, "Moon Man."

But he didn't think that was funny at all when I came over to tell him about the moon. You couldn't say too much to him on the field. I remember one time I booted a ball in Boston in the 1967 World Series against the Red Sox when I was trying to get it on the short hop, and it bounced out of my glove. I'm moaning over there, and he said, "Give me the damn ball."

And he struck the next two guys out. But there weren't too many Gibsons around. He said that he didn't ever mean to hit anybody. He hit 102 guys. And I guarantee you he meant to hit most of them. He didn't slip 102 times.

And by the way, he won two games in that 1964 World Series, including the seventh game pitching on two days' rest. That was after he won Game Five pitching 10 innings in Yankee Stadium when McCarver homered in the 10th inning. That game came one day after we got back in the World Series when Ken Boyer hit a grand slam, and our bullpen held on for a 4–3 win in Game Four to even it at two games apiece.

There were so many highlights in that World Series. Our starter, Ray Sadecki, was knocked out in the first inning of Game Four when the Yankees got off to a 3–0 lead. But Roger Craig and Ron Taylor out of our bullpen held the Yankees to two hits and struck out 10 over the final eight-and-two-thirds innings. If the Yankees had won that game, it might have been all over. As it turned out, they didn't win another World Series until 1977.

In Game Five Gibson had made a tremendous play on Joe Pepitone in the ninth inning, whirling and throwing him out from the third-base foul line after a smash had gone off his leg. That play preceded a two-out homer by Tom Tresh, which would have won the game if it hadn't been for Gibson's great play.

I was a kid along for the ride with all these great veterans like Boyer and Dick Groat. Curt Simmons and Bill White. Bob Skinner and Curt Flood. And then, of course, there were Gibson and Lou Brock, who were at the heart of the matter.

There wasn't nearly as much talk on the field in those days as there is now. That was very much frowned upon. But guys like Ernie Banks, who was playing first base for the Cubs, was always chattering. Our shortstop, Dal Maxvill, asked me, "Does Banks talk to you when you get on first base?"

I said, "Yeah, all the time."

"You want to shut him up?" Maxie said. "Just mention to him that all his home runs end up in the first row of seats behind the wall."

So I did, and he shut up from then on. But he kept hitting three-run homers, and I said, "Somebody's got to hit that guy." And somebody did. And Banks didn't play the next day.

I said, "Ernie, how come you're not playing?"

"You hit me," he said. "I'll just get the next team."

Mission accomplished. That's what it was designed to do.

But nobody had more fun than Banks. If I'd hit 500 home runs, I would have had a good time, too. That's like Stan Musial. If I had hit .330 every year, I would have been a nice guy, too.

Before I became a regular for those three World Series teams in 1964, 1967, and 1968, I was up and down between the minors and the big leagues three different times. Experience got me every time. One year I got to camp, and the Cardinals traded for George Altman from the Cubs. That was it for me at the start of that season. Altman had hit 27 homers and then 22 for the Cubs in 1961–62, but he had just nine for us in 1963. Still, that was a year that was taken away from me. Altman got traded to the Mets in 1964.

That, of course, was the first season after Musial had retired after his 22-season career. If he hadn't done that, there wouldn't have been any place for me or Gary Kolb. And eventually, when I got my chance, I played hard. You could ask Glenn Beckert, who played second for the Cubs. There was a time when a bunch of players decided we wouldn't sign our personal contracts when Marvin Miller, who was head of the players' association and who finally went into the Hall of Fame in 2020, was looking for some leverage. But about two weeks later, Beckert signed his contract. I didn't like that. When I had a chance, I ran into him at second base. He knew it, and I knew it. Nobody else knew it. It wasn't anybody else's business but his and mine. I took it personally when he told me he had signed his contract.

I hit a home run in each of the three World Series I played in. One was at the old Busch Stadium and the other two—in 1967 and 1968—at the new Busch Stadium, which had opened in May of 1966. At the old one, I had the last Cardinals home run on May 8. At the new one, I had the first Cardinals hit on May 12 and the first Cardinals home run the next day.

I was an outfielder when I got to the major leagues in 1962, but much of my time ended up being spent at third base, where I moved in 1967 when we got Roger Maris from the Yankees. I went over there because I knew we had a lot of outfielders but not really any third basemen. Baseball teams often have only one third baseman. He plays every day no matter what. I went over there because of the security of it. I asked Maxvill if I should do it, and he said, "No, you should stay where you are." But I still did it.

Everyone wanted Maxxie to put on weight, but I told him—and he weighed about 155 pounds—if he put on weight, he wouldn't be able to catch the ground balls. "That's your strength," I said to him. "Don't ever take away your strength."

He was never going to be able to hit anyway because he always moved his back foot when he was hitting. If it hadn't been for some guy getting hurt in the minor leagues, Maxie wouldn't have been in the big leagues in the first place. But you can say that about a lot of guys. Right time, right place.

I replaced Charley Smith at third base. He had a rough ride because he wasn't Boyer, the great third baseman on our 1964 World Series champions. After Boyer was traded to the Mets following the 1965 season, Smith lasted just one year with us, hitting .266 with 10 homers and 43 RBIs. So when I took over, I wasn't really replacing Boyer, per se. But it's not the person you're replacing that's as important as the position. That's extremely important.

They took me out to Forest Park in St. Louis in the offseason, and coach Joe Schultz hit me a bunch of ground balls. Then the late, great George Kissell and others ran me through my paces in Florida at spring training. Later on, Kissell would do the same for Joe Torre and Andy Van Slyke and a few others. He would have you out there in the early morning and hit ground ball after ground ball to you. And then you would start your regular spring training day. Teaching is one of the most difficult things there is. I don't care what industry you're in. Kissell might be the best teacher ever. It was a gift.

I didn't always know where to play position-wise, though, during games. I would ask Gibson when he was pitching where he wanted me to play. He said, "Don't worry about it. Most times I'm not going to let them hit the ball to you. But if there's a guy at first and it's a double-play potential, then I'll make them hit it to you."

Well, the next 10 guys in those situations hit the ball on one hop to me. *Boom. Boom. Boom.* Ten double plays. It didn't make a lot of sense when he said it at the time. After a while I analyzed what he meant, and it made so much sense. He would throw that two-seamer inside to a right-handed hitter and try to get him to hit a one-hopper to third base, where I was playing. He had such phenomenal control. That's why he was Bob Gibson. I didn't realize a pitcher could make a hitter hit the ball exactly where the pitcher wanted.

One of the things about Gibby was that I always thought he wanted to succeed because he was afraid of not succeeding. He said he didn't think that. But he was sickly as a kid in Omaha, Nebraska, with all kinds of diseases and he got his butt kicked all the time. Then he grew up and developed into a man, and I thought losing was more of a thing to him than winning was. But when I told him that, he got all ticked off.

He sure didn't lose too much. I felt good about hitting a homer in Busch Stadium in each of three World Series in which I played, but he won seven games in those series, including the clincher in 1964 against the Yankees and three games against Boston in 1967. But I'm still ticked off about 1968 when we lost to Detroit after leading three games to one. The Tigers were a damn good club.

The key to the series was when Mayo Smith, the Detroit manager, let Mickey Lolich bat for himself with his team down a run and one out and nobody on in the seventh inning of the fifth game. We had a 3–2 lead and were three innings from winning the series. We probably should have been further ahead, but Brock had been called out on a close play at the plate when he didn't slide as he tried to score from second on a single by Julian Javier. But he was safe. I saw it. Umpire Doug Harvey, who ultimately went into the Hall of Fame with Whitey Herzog, called Brock out.

I know why Smith left Lolich in to hit. Every time we got to that bullpen, we lit that bullpen up like it was a damn candle. Lolich was a terrible hitter. But Mayo himself had said, "Every time I took Lolich out, the bullpen let it go." So he had an excuse. And it turned the whole series around.

Of course, Lolich got a hit off Nelson Briles, Detroit scored three runs in the inning and won that game. Then they won the next two, including clobbering us 13–1 at Busch Stadium in Game Six.

I homered for our only run off Lolich with two out in the ninth inning of Game Seven. The game had been scoreless into the seventh before Flood slipped in center field chasing a ball that Jim Northrup hit that became a game-deciding, two-run triple. Gibson suffered the loss in what would be his and my final World Series game. But he finished 7–2 in the World Series. We still had some more ball to play. We went over to Japan to play a series of exhibition games, and I hit three home runs in one game, which was one of the highlights of my career that really didn't count.

People would ask me, "What's the difference between your team and my team?"

My answer was simple: "Gibson. We'd get to a World Series, and he'd win three games. We knew we just had to win one."

Those were the best times. All you can think about as a kid is batting with the bases loaded in the seventh game of the World Series. It didn't happen quite like that, but three World Series in five years is pretty good. I got to broadcast some World Series, too, but it's not the same. It's one-on-one when you're playing.

People wondered if I felt any pressure playing at home, where you'd look in the stands and think you knew everyone and that everybody knew you. But it was never a problem for me. I had played almost my whole athletic career in St. Louis, so why should it be any different when I got to the big leagues?

I even caught a few games, and that was an experience. The first came on August 8, 1965. I had never caught anywhere—not in amateur ball, college, or the minors. But we're playing the Giants. McCarver was already out, and Bob

Uecker split his thumb catching a foul tip from the Giants' Dick Schofield, the first batter in the game. We didn't have any other catchers, and Red Schoendienst, our manager, asked me if I wanted to catch. I asked him if I was going to get three at-bats.

I didn't even know how to put the shin guards on. I never had had them on before. I hooked them up wrong, of course, and when I tried to walk, they caught each other. I had to use Uecker's catcher's mitt, and there was about an inch of Uecker's blood in there, which I had to pour out. McCarver was hurt and wasn't there, and I never thought to ask Uecker if he had another glove.

But the good thing was that Curt Simmons was the pitcher, and you can catch him without a glove. It was probably better than catching Gibson, though I did play with Gibson in a fantasy camp game after a regular Cardinals game about 20 years later. I ticked him off by missing a foul pop-up on purpose so that Bob Costas could get another at-bat. Gibson said, "What are you doing?"

I said that I wanted to give him another chance. Gibson responded, "Screw him."

Then Costas hit a liner to left center. It was 1984, and Brock and Flood had lost a step, and the ball went for a triple on the AstroTurf. Costas said, "Gibson was not amused.

Only half-kidding, Gibson said that if I had come up again, he would have knocked me on my rear."

The first hitter Simmons faced with me catching—Jesus Alou—hit a home run. Simmons said, "The next time he comes up, I'm going to knock him down."

And he did. That was the first time I was ever on the good part of a knockdown.

But, later, I tagged out Willie Mays at the plate and then threw to third to get Jim Ray Hart for a double play. And I had a double and a triple and I caught my first knuckleballer in Barney Schultz. I had a little tip from pitcher Lew Burdette about it. He said, "Don't try to catch it until it stops moving."

I did all right that day, but Billy Williams was the home-plate umpire and he wasn't so sure. He asked me if I had ever caught before, and I could see the look on his face and how scared he was when he heard that I hadn't. But then all my fear left me.

I went out to Simmons and said, "What do you want to use for signs?"

He said, "Fingers."

I said, "Okay, I've got five of those. How many pitches do you have?" He said he had four. I said, "Good."

But then I looked back at Williams about the fourth or the fifth inning and I saw that fear back on his face again. Schultz was warming up.

I had never caught in Little League or high school or college or anywhere, but maybe catching should have been my calling. The first game I started as a catcher was four days later and I hit a home run in Milwaukee when we beat the Braves in 13 innings with me catching the first 12 of them. But I got tired after catching so long, and there were some balls going by me in the later innings.

I will say that when I went to third base a couple of years later, that catching deal helped me there. What you learn to do by catching is to pay attention to the fundamentals and not the baseball. All of a sudden, the fundamentals become natural, and you can concentrate on the ball.

I liked it because the catcher is the only guy on the field who is looking out. You could see everything that was going on. And the game doesn't really start until you put your finger down. I always enjoyed that part of it because the psychological part of baseball was what interested me anyway.

I could have caught more, but they said that I was an outfielder and a third baseman. But when I retired in 1970, I would have basically been three players. I played the outfield and the infield and I could catch, so they could have saved two spots on the roster or least the backup catcher spot.

I got along with everybody on those Cardinals teams whether he was Black or White. When you're playing with a guy, you don't care if he's Black, White, pink, or polka dotted. It never enters your thoughts. You just want to know if you can get in a foxhole with him. We had four great Black players in White, Flood, Brock, and Gibson. They were all great citizens besides being great baseball players. But you look at the citizen part of it when they're done playing.

Gibson always was fun to talk to because he always had a different perspective. Everybody thought of him as a guy who had that great stuff, but he was very intelligent. It's like he told me—just be ready when there's a man at first and nobody out or one out. I learned a lot from him on the field and I learned a lot from Lew Burdette off the field.

The club assigned me to room with Burdette, who was a night owl much as I would become. One time we're in Milwaukee, where he used to play, and he said we were going to see Jerry Lee Lewis perform in an old foundry that had been renovated. He said, "Roomie, we're going to have a treat tonight."

Hell, I was a rookie. I couldn't afford to go anywhere. The only thing I knew about Jerry Lee was that he got up on the piano and beat on it. That night, he got up on the piano and he beat it with his shoe and his fist. It was a hell of a show.

Yeah, I learned a lot all right from Burdette, whom I roomed with in 1962 and 1963. One time he came in late in San Francisco, and we had to get up early. He said, "Roomie, get me up at 10 in the morning."

And then he passed out. I tried to undress him and everything and get him in bed and I was able to get him up in the morning. We made the airplane. I don't know who put us together, but it turned out all right. His habits were worse than mine. He had a lot of experience. Let's put it that way. I was a choirboy compared to him.

Before the 1968 World Series, we had been very much aware of the Tigers. They had Denny McLain, who won 31 games that year, but Maris, who had played against Detroit a lot in the American League, said, "McLain's not the guy who's going to get us. The guy who is going to get us is Lolich." And he was right. Roger was a smart guy.

We had a lot of smart guys on those teams. We never beat ourselves. Schoendienst, who was our manager on those 1967 and 1968 clubs, let us play. All he wanted was for us to show up on time and play. We didn't have any problems with it. Our general manager in 1965 and 1966 was Bob Howsam, who had a lot of quirky things about him that weren't traditional baseball, but he was still the boss. I came to the ballpark in June of 1966, and Schoendienst said that the general manager wanted to see me. Howsam had this idea that if you were struggling, he would send you to the minor leagues to get your hitting eye back. I wasn't playing. I was hitting .228. But I told Schoendienst, "Don't give my uniform away. I'll be back."

I figured I'd try to talk Howsam out of it and I did. I came back and told Schoendienst, "I'm back on your team."

So the next day we're playing the Giants and Juan Marichal, and I'm in the lineup. I figured I was the sacrificial lamb. And then we went out to Los Angeles to face all those great pitchers they had. I wound up being the Player of the Month for the National League for July. I saved my whole career in the big leagues.

It was like Schoendienst had said, "Okay, we'll see if that kid can hit." He had looked at the schedule. Marichal. Sandy Koufax. Don Drysdale...

I went hitless against Marichal on June 29, but then when we got to Los Angeles, I hit a two-run homer off Koufax; tripled off Drysdale two days later; and on the Fourth of July, I hit a two-run homer off Marichal in San Francisco. I hit .395 for the month, I had 45 hits, and I had a 5-for-5 game in Chicago. I just got hot at the right time. Again, right place at the right time. I ended the year with my career-best .288 average.

Later in his career, when Schoendienst wasn't managing but was a consultant with the team, he was amazing at judging talent. He could take one look at a guy and know what he was going to do. On our bed checks when Schoendienst was managing, he just wanted to make sure the beds were there. We didn't necessarily have to be in them. Hell, he had done this all himself when he was playing. But with all the crazy stuff they did together on the road, he and Stan Musial always would seem to get six hits in a doubleheader.

We were going to San Francisco on one trip and we stopped over in Las Vegas. I had a friend who ran one of the hotels there, and we had Gibson pitching, and everybody bet on San Francisco because they got a good betting line with Gibson pitching. Naturally, Gibson shut them out. They had been sending drinks and some other stuff to our rooms the night before, but Gibson was pitching. It was a different story when he pitched.

But there was at least one time when we didn't help him at all. We had just clinched the pennant in Houston in 1968 and when we got to San Francisco on that Sunday night we had a party out on California Street. It just happened to be a long one. I remember Joe Hoerner, our closer, had put a hole in the inner glass of the airplane on our flight to San Francisco, and the party already had started. This is the same guy that commandeered the team bus once in Atlanta, and somebody said, "You may not be able to make it under that overpass."

He said, "If I get up enough speed, I will."

He made it just under the bridge. There couldn't have been an inch's difference. And he was the guy who once told a priest, "Oh, Father, every time I see you, I feel like I have to go to confession for all the cursing I did when I was on the mound."

The priest said, "That's all right. I curse a lot when you're on the mound, too."

We partied all night in San Francisco and part of the next day, too. Then we had an afternoon game on Tuesday with the Giants and Gaylord Perry pitching for them against Gibson. We were a little hungover, maybe a lot hungover, and we got no-hit as Gibson lost 1–0. He was not very happy. The next day, then, we made up for it. Ray Washburn no-hit the Giants, and we beat them 2–0. I had two of our seven hits and drove in a run.

But we had the most fun in Chicago because we played all day games. I used to come back from the game, order room service for dinner, take a nap, and then go out again about midnight. One time I came back in and I called the operator and said, "Call me at 8:00."

I hung up, and no sooner had I done that, the phone rang, and the operator said, "It's 8:00."

I said, "What time did I call you?"

She said, "Just a minute ago."

But it didn't bother me. Kissell always called me the exception to the rule. He said, "You can't soar with the eagles if you're hanging with the turkeys."

New York was one of my favorite places. I used to hang out with "Big Julie" Isaacson and we'd go to the race track a lot. He was head of the Toymakers' Union, which was the second largest union in the nation behind the Teamsters. I don't know how powerful a guy he was, but he said one time, "The East River is full. So we've got to think of something else."

I didn't ask any questions.

In San Francisco I spent a lot of time with Billy Breslin, who was president of the Olympic Club. I didn't have too much to worry about with Big Julie and the president of the Olympic Club. Lon Simmons, the broadcaster of the Giants, told me, "I've been around here for 27 years, and you've got more influence than I do."

We had fun; I know that. Once Maris and I stole that famous St. Bernard that was out in front of a popular Chinese restaurant in San Francisco and took the dog into another restaurant, and there was a dog under the table that I didn't see. They just growled at each other. They didn't fight, but the guy, who had the other dog, was comedian George Carlin, and he got mad and left. I had to apologize to the guy who ran the restaurant. I can remember putting that dog back into a cab, and the St. Bernard was slobbering all over the cab driver.

Maris and I used to have a blast. He knew the great Joe DiMaggio from his days with the Yankees, and every time we got to San Francisco, where the Yankee Clipper had a restaurant, he would have Dungeness crab waiting for Maris at the hotel. Joe D. gave me a great interview my first year in broadcasting in 1972 in Atlanta. Maris came to the team before the 1967 season, and before that I had spent a lot of time with Bob Skinner, who had played on the 1960 World Series champion Pittsburgh Pirates and for us in 1964. One thing I asked him was why the Pirates seemed to have so many good pinch hitters, including him. He said, "The pitcher gets one pitch, the umpire gets one, and you get one." But you didn't ask him stupid questions. Or you would get a stupid answer.

Skinner had good baseball sense, and whenever I needed help, I asked him who I should see. He told me to see Don Hoak with the Pirates, and he helped me when I went to play third base. I knew if I stayed with the fundamentals, I'd be all right. Three days before the games started, balls were flying by me left and right, but I knew if I stayed with the fundamentals, it would come to me. Before that, I wasn't paying attention to the ball. You've got to pay attention to the ball, you know? Which comes first? The chicken or the egg? You know it's the egg because that's where the chicken comes from. But sometimes it doesn't work that way. All I know is that you'd better be ready because when you cross those white lines, that ball will find you.

The veteran players would give you a good answer to a question, but you might have to wait a few years. I had trouble hitting Drysdale because I couldn't see the ball off him. I knew I couldn't hit the damn guy. But I didn't know why. Later on, I asked Torre how he hit Drysdale so well and he said, "I just look at his right knee."

I said, "Well, you could have told me that a few years ago. It's too late now."

But I knew Drysdale was finished when a ball slipped out of his hand and he said, "Whoops."

I got a triple off the left-field wall. You can't get a triple in Dodger Stadium off the left-field wall, but they were so surprised I hit it that they didn't know what to do.

With Koufax it was a little bit different. I hit eighth when I first came up, and he wouldn't mess with me. Just fastballs. I eliminated his curveball when I had two strikes. I just tried to let the ball hit my bat. I looked for his fastball high and outside of the box, and one day in LA, he hit my bat. I beat him 2–1 with a home run in the eighth inning. The next time I faced him, he threw me a fastball inside. I stepped out of the batter's box, and I said to the catcher, John Roseboro, "We've got a new game here, don't we?"

Rosey said, "I think you ticked the Big Jew off." You could say things like that then. Those were irreverent times.

I remember that voice in my head that said, "Fastball. Fastball inside." That's why I was always out in front of the ball all the time—that little guy whispering in my ear. It took me a long time to figure that stuff out.

One of the guys I had the most trouble with was little reliever Elroy Face of Pittsburgh, a great right-hander who finished his career with the Montreal Expos. He had that forkball, and I would swing at it two or three times—on the same pitch—and still never hit it. Then, in the ninth inning of a game in late June in 1969, I hit a three-run homer off him, and it wasn't too long after that that he retired.

Schoendienst once told me to raise my bat when I was hitting. I did that, but I said, "Why did it take you six years to tell me?"

But when somebody asked Schoendienst which hitter he would want up there with the game on the line, he said it was me. I said, "Not Musial or Albert Pujols?"

He said no. I knew what they were going to throw me, I guess. But I know that one year I had a lot of game-winning RBIs because I had all those gift certificates to Holiday Inn. Back then, you got rewarded with "Star of the Game" gift certificates, and all those RBIs sure played a role in me getting those. I could take my family down to the Ozarks, and we could use the Holiday Inn gift certificates down there.

I didn't have many theories about how to achieve success, but I did operate under the philosophy that sleeping is bad for you. I'm no kinesiologist by any stretch, but I still think it's overrated how much sleep you get. You can sleep all you want when they're getting ready to put that stuff in the ground for when you're going to take that long dirt nap. When I would go to sleep, the first two hours I'd be asleep, you could put me on a stretcher, take me to the airport, fly me to the next city, and I wouldn't have even known it. I slept hard. I watched Musial. He took naps. That what's I do now. If Musial got in line to buy horse manure, I'd be second in line.

When I played, there were a lot more day games. But when I began broadcasting, baseball was starting to play a lot more night games and I would have time to go to the track in the afternoon in some of the cities. You have so much more time as a broadcaster than as a player. That's why I kind of took the job in the first place because you kind of make your own schedule.

In Cincinnati, you can rest except if you wanted to go across the Ohio River. There were lot of places that stayed open late in Newport and Covington, Kentucky. There were no rules. There were plenty of towns to rest in. But there were also New York, Chicago, and San Francisco. Those were towns where you could have some fun.

We had a golf date in Los Angeles that Vin Scully had set up at his course. Jack Buck, who was playing, wasn't among the best of golfers. As sophisticated as he was on the air, he wasn't very sophisticated on the golf course. He used to walk in your line. He said something to the caddy like, "You may be the worst caddy in the world."

And without missing a beat, the caddy replied, "That would be too much of a coincidence." I had to turn away because it was so funny. It was hilarious.

The players of today don't have as much fun as we did. There's too much money involved. Guys are making $20 million a year; they've got to take care of themselves. Twenty million dollars? Can you imagine that? I was the third highest-paid third baseman in the game when I retired. I was behind only Ron Santo and Brooks Robinson and I had played in three World Series. But I made $52,500 at my highest.

Later, when I was broadcasting, I wanted to interview Mike Schmidt, and he started talking about me. I said I don't want to talk about me. I said, "Stop the tape. I want to talk about you."

But he said, "I admired you because you had so much fun."

I said, "Oh, you hit over 500 home runs and you didn't have any fun?"

People called me a "character," and others have tried to impersonate me and my broadcasting style and some of the things that I had said on the air. Well, they say the utmost flattery is to be imitated. That's the way I took it. But the players before—and they may now, too—can have fun at the expense of a rookie. Or they can make it difficult for that rookie to have fun. Al Kaline, the great Detroit outfielder, came out of high school right to the big leagues, and they didn't like him at all because he took one of their buddies' spots.

It's a little harder now to do stuff outside the ballpark with everybody having a cell phone, and people taking pictures of you. It's pretty hard to have fun—in public anyway.

Uecker was one of the funniest guys I played with and as an announcer, too. He's still doing the Milwaukee Brewers games at age 88. Before the first game of the 1964 World Series in St. Louis, Uecker was trying to catch baseballs in a tuba, which belonged to Bob Kuban and the In-Men, a band that was performing that day. But Johnny Keane, the manager, didn't like that and didn't play him in the entire seven-game series. Schoendienst told Uecker about Keane's anger about 20 years later, and Ueck, who never had been told the reason why he didn't play, got mad.

Uecker was a good catcher and he could hit those left-handers pretty well. One night Koufax stuck one in his ribs.

I never knew what that term meant until Uecker went down to the ground, and the ball just rolled off of him.

We probably had more characters in the game than we do now. Joe Hoerner had to throw sidearm because he had this heart condition. They said if he raised his arm over his heart, he would have a heart attack. He was a man. They tell a story about him cleaning a bar out in Texas. There were a couple of cowboys fighting, and they bumped into him, and he got upset. So he threw everybody out, but then he went back outside and said, "Which one of you guys is the bartender?" One of the guys put his hand up, and Hoerner said, "You can come back in."

He wanted to fight this one guy on our own team. It was Richie Allen. I didn't think it was a good idea. I said, "We can always get another relief pitcher, but we never can get another Richie Allen."

Allen was with us only one year, but he was something. He had come from Philadelphia and when he got to us, he said, "I think I'll just turn it up a notch."

The first night, he sent a ball about 30 rows up in the right-center-field bleachers. He wasn't the most punctual of players, though. He would show up late for games. (Alcohol may have been involved sometimes,) and Schoendienst would have two different lineups ready. One time we're in Philadelphia, where he lived until he passed away in 2020, and Allen's wife drove him to the game, and the clubhouse guy told Schoendienst just before the game started that Allen was there. Schoendienst put him in the lineup, and he hit two homers. Just as the game ended, Schoendienst told "Ace," the clubhouse attendant, "Get that guy dressed and get him out of here before the press gets here."

Allen was big into horses, and that occupied him most of his time in his retirement. I, too, used to own a horse. She was named Miss Susan's Rib, and I really liked it. She won the biggest two-year-old filly race in Illinois, a $100,000 race. After I bought that horse in February, I told the guy, who was over at Fairmount Park, a local track just across the river from St. Louis, that I was going to win that big race. And I did. But that was six months down the road. A lot can happen in six months with horses in three days, let alone six months. She won a couple of stakes races and then, sure enough, got hurt.

The players today are better athletes than we were. They're better athletes, but they're not better players. The difference is that they don't have the experience. Before guys played in the minor leagues for a long time, and when they came to the big leagues, they already knew how to play. Look at how many kids make the team out of spring training. That never used to happen 20 years ago. You went to spring training, and there maybe was one spot open where you could make the team. How many guys did Musial keep in the minor leagues? Mo Mozzali, my first manager in Class D ball, used to hit .350 every year and he had no chance as an outfielder to beat out Musial, who was hitting .330 in the big leagues.

I didn't think much about my playing career after I stopped playing, though I could have stayed in uniform as a minor league manager. I had five kids, and my wife had taken care of me when I was sick, and I couldn't see leaving her again. And they would be even worse hours. So I had to turn it down. I don't regret turning down the managing job. At the time, it was the right thing to do. Would I have been a good manager? Who knows? The time was just never right, you know? Sometimes decisions are made for you instead of you making decisions.

I do everything long term but also day by day. In other words, I went into the restaurant business later on and I intended to be in it the rest of my life. Whatever I was doing, I made decisions for a lifetime, not just a week or a month or a year or whatever.

Things still went the right way, and there I was 50 years later doing the broadcasts. The good thing about broadcasting was that I could make up my own hours, and it would be easier on my wife. I made all my decisions based on my wife and my family. Basically, it was easy to make those decisions because they were kind of made for me. In 1972 Mike was the oldest and he was 10 years old. We had five then, and Eric came along later. Did I like broadcasting right away? I don't know. I just kind of took to it, or it took to me, or it was a combination of the two. I just realized it was an opportunity and I had to capitalize on it if I was going to do anything in baseball. So I don't know if it picked me, or I picked it.

My father was a good athlete and he was on the police force while he was studying for a law degree at Washington University in St. Louis. He was at the top of his class for criminal law. But he never went into criminal law. He became a city prosecutor for 22 or 23 years. The thing I learned most from him was that you make your own decisions and you live with them and show up on time. There's something to be said about punctuality. And character. That's a word we don't use very much now these days. It still means something to me. He used to come watch me play. But he would sit all the way down the right-field line instead of sitting behind home plate and yelling at the umpire.

When I got sick with kidney disease, the trainer wanted to wait a day or two before we made the announcement that I was done. But Dr. Stan London said, "You can wait all you want. But he's not putting a uniform on."

That took a lot of guts. Especially for a first-year guy as he was. That told me he had character.

BOB UECKER

Mike Shannon didn't have an impact on me, thank God. If I had had to hang around him every day, I probably would have been in an institution. If you ever wanted to do something to somebody and tick them off, you could put him in the booth with Mike for a whole game.

But, no, Mike and I always had a good relationship. We always had a lot of fun. We used to go fishing on our trips in there. And I'd either go with Red Schoendienst or the Moon Man. I was Mike's teammate in 1964–65, and later we both became radio voices for teams in the same division. Shannon was there as a player with the World Series championships and he had an impact on a game—like with his cannon of a throwing arm. For example, knowing what it was like to be in a clubhouse where you had lost 10 in a row and everybody wants to know what's going on, that gives you a little different perspective as a broadcaster. Nobody can tell you what it is because you know. You played. You were there.

He even caught. I remember a series in Chicago where I got my foot caught in that gutter behind home plate along the dugout and wall in Wrigley Field. I got my foot in there and twisted it, and Shannon went in and caught. He could do anything. He didn't care. And he could run, too.

He didn't get that nickname—Moon Man—for nothing. And Mike wasn't shy about anything. He was a different individual. He was one of those unique guys who comes along every once in a while, hangs around, becomes a friend of everybody, and they believe what he says. It goes back even to high school in St. Louis where he was a big star. It goes back that far with him. It warrants credibility. It really does. You can't make an excuse for something you screwed up on the field, and a guy like Mike is going to tell the people why a play didn't get made.

I'll miss him on the circuit. I always got a laugh out of talking to him. I used to give him pieces of black cloth that I had so he could patch that black jacket he always had. He had that black jacket for 100 years. He dressed the same all the time. Years ago, when we had to wear shirts and ties, he'd wear a tie with that crappy jacket. He might have one brown shoe and one black shoe. He didn't care.

CHAPTER 5

Broadcasting

The broadcasting job kept me away from home a lot but not as much as a coach or manager would be gone. And it's even worse for those broadcasters now than it was back then. The way the game is played now—everything is more drastic. For instance, how many times does the shift work? I try to explain on the air, but basically I don't believe in it.

For people who ask me if broadcasting was fun right away, I tell them I don't do things unless they're fun. So, I guess right away it probably was. I kind of play everything by ear. If it works, it works. If it doesn't, it doesn't. And I took the broadcasting job the same way. I don't change—good or bad. You have to be yourself. The listeners are very intelligent people. I don't think you can fool them by pretending you're somebody you're not.

I still had plenty to learn like the fundamentals that the producer/engineer wanted, such as when they wanted a spot to be read. It's like playing. It's the fundamentals. The fundamentals were the hardest thing, just like in any job. If you stay with them, they will work. But I had no idea how any of those things worked. Nowadays, it seems as if everything in the game is sponsored by somebody. The lineups, the first pitch—you just had to weave it into the game, even though technically it wasn't part of the game. I told Joe Buck that it wouldn't be too long before "this home run is brought to you by such and such."

And he said, "Really?"

Everything is sponsored now. When the topic of the National Anthem being sponsored came up, I told them they had to get a new broadcaster if that was going to be sponsored. And they never talked about it again. At least, not yet.

As a broadcaster one of the hardest things I had to concentrate on at first was: "dese, dose, and dem" from the German influence that I had growing up in St. Louis. You had to say, "these, those, and them." They sent me over to the Central Institute for the Deaf, and a guy worked with me. It's a matter of using proper mechanics with your mouth to say, "these, those, and them."

It was kind of like baseball. When I went from the outfield to third base, I paid attention to the fundamentals because only two days before the game, balls were going by me left and right. I knew that if I just concentrated on the fundamentals, it would come into play. I first learned that when they had me go down to work on my catching with Vern Rapp, a catching instructor who later became our manager in 1977. Concentrating on the fundamentals helped get me through those first few years, but they didn't help me get along any better with Rapp when he was managing. I went into his office one day to ask him about something and I said the answer was better that it came from him than me. He said, "Well, that's a stupid question."

I said, "I know it is."

He said, "I'm still not going to answer it [on the air]."

I knew he was going to get fired (in 1978) when he wouldn't go on the air. He was supposed to go on the air on KMOX because of the deal with pitcher Al Hrabosky, who had this big Fu Manchu and long hair but had been told to shave. I said, "Who do you want to answer those questions? Somebody else or you?" He said he didn't want to answer those questions anymore so I knew he was going to get fired.

That's just like I knew Red Schoendienst was going to get fired as manager before they hired Rapp. Stan Musial, Schoendienst's lifelong friend and confidant, wasn't invited to a meeting of the top officials one time in 1976, and without Musial to stand up for Schoendienst, I knew that was going to be the end for Schoendienst. I called him and said, "Hey, Red, you want to go have a drink?" We had just gotten rained out in Pittsburgh, and I said, "You're going to get fired tomorrow."

He was going to get fired a lot of times, but Musial always saved him.

You learn as you go along. And sitting next to Jack Buck in the booth, well, he was a professional. All I had to do—if I was smart—was to keep my mouth shut and my eyes and ears open. I had the good fortune of working with a Hall of Famer so I paid attention to what he said and what he did. I watched and listened. At least I was that smart. I knew this was a hell of an opportunity. But he didn't coddle me. He threw me the play-by-play one day and said he wasn't going to do all of it anymore. That's the only way you're going to learn anything in life. You just jump in. You'll find out pretty quickly if you can handle it.

Jack was a phenomenal guy, very patient. He would give me little hints along the way. Basically, I had on-the-job training. I partnered with Jack for 30 years. I was smart enough to know how he was received and I just saw how he worked. I learned so much from him. It's kind of osmosis. It just rubs off. Jack's great asset was that he knew how something was going to sound before he said it. But a lot of other guys I worked with were great, too. Everybody's different. And I still did it my way.

Jack only gave me two pieces of advice. Don't eat popcorn. And when the home-plate umpire had a new supply of baseballs, you should say "baseballs." You don't say, "There's a new supply of balls for the plate umpire." Those are the only things he ever told me.

But he never missed a chance to tease me, too. For one of our early broadcasts, he told me to go get the umpires. He likes to tell the story that I actually brought them up to the booth. He did like to embellish things a little.

Then, for my first spring game in St. Petersburg, Florida, the other team had a guy named Kurt Bevacqua. He had an eye chart for a name. So I asked Jack, "How do you pronounce this guy's name?"

And he said, "Buh-VOK-qua." I practiced it over and over, and we went on the air, and Jack said, "This is Jack Buck from St. Petersburg, Florida, and Mike Shannon's favorite player [Bevacqua] is here today." That was Jack. He didn't mind throwing a guy into the fire, and we went from there.

We always got along great, though I didn't know Jack that well when I was playing. Harry Caray was the lead broadcaster then, so you had a lot more to do with him. Caray was fine unless you were Kenny Boyer, and you popped out to end the game. He would snap after a key Boyer at-bat in the ninth inning, "Popped it up. Totals and highlights in a minute."

Did I like all my partners? Let's just say that I had partners I liked better, but I've liked all of them by and large. Joe Buck, as far as I was concerned, had more talent than anybody I ever worked with. Tremendous talent. And he had a lot of gumption, too, a lot of intestinal fortitude. There comes a time when you have to say no, and he knew how to do that. He was very good at that. But he had more talent than anybody, including his father. He was—and still is—a tremendous broadcaster. He, like me, saw the merits of working with his father and he took advantage of that.

We had quite a collection of sports broadcasters at KMOX radio in St. Louis, including one of the great hockey announcers, Dan Kelly of the St. Louis Blues, who did some St. Louis Cardinals games. But Kelly didn't have any confidence in his baseball skills. So one day I said, "Dan, if I came to hockey, would you take care of me?"

And he said, "Sure."

I said, "Well, damn it, relax. Just be yourself. I'll take care of you."

I remember he went down to the field in Montreal to do the Star of the Game show, but he was about 20 minutes late. The producer asked me what we should do, and I said, "Let's do it anyway."

We weren't even on the air. But Kelly had gotten lost, which was understandable in that ballpark. You didn't know if you were inside or outside—or even in the right place because they had that velodrome right next to Olympic Stadium.

At the start of my career, I was just being me, but it probably took five or six years to get comfortable. If they wanted me to be something else, well, they didn't have a choice. I know I've had some head-scratching lines over the years, but there was always a method behind my madness. But when stuff happened like I said it was going to happen, then they paid attention.

One of the lines I used a lot was "Ol' Abner's done it again," referring to Abner Doubleday, who gets credit for inventing the game of baseball as we know it, though he probably didn't really invent it. I don't think anybody else has used that line. It just came to me. A lot of the stuff I came up was spontaneous. I did not consider myself much of a planner. I would react to what I saw. I liked saying for a pitch over the heart of the plate, "Right down central."

I got panned for some of the things I said on the air, and people would repeat them with a smile, but I looked at it as imitation is the greatest form of flattery.

Some of my most interesting lines were:

- "Well, that's the life of a reliever. It's either a mountain or a valley. There's no in-between. You either get all of the glory or all of the goat hair."

- "Acevedo tried to sneak that pitch past Pujols on the inside corner. That's like trying to sneak the sun past the rooster."
- "Everyone's on a pitch count now. You people down on the farms don't let Major League Baseball on your place, or they will have the cows on a pitch count."
- Of a game in Montreal, "This game is moving along pretty quick. It must have something to do with the exchange rate."
- Referring to a young fan who was hit with a foul ball, "That youngster will leave the stadium with a souvenir today. Not a ball but a nice-looking bruise."
- "This game is off to a rather conspicuous start, don't you think, Jack?"

I've had some great moments on the air. Once during a tight situation, I said the Cardinals were looking for a triple play. Sure enough, there was a line drive to Albert Pujols, who turned the triple play. "Ask and you shall receive," I said on the air.

The "Get up, baby, get up, baby!" for home runs came from Mark McGwire's 70th on the final day of the season. It was a line drive that barely cleared the left-field wall. "Seventy home runs. Take a ride on that for history" was the rest of that call.

But my favorite might have been a July 4 home run Pujols hit off Chicago Cubs pitcher Kerry Wood in Wrigley Field after Wood had knocked Pujols down with the previous pitch. The KMOX call was like this: "Wouldn't I love to see [home run] No. 25 off Albert's bat go into the street? Swing...and hello, Fourth of July, take a ride on that knockdown pitch, big boy...Take a little whiff of that big boy...Give it to him, big boy, give it to him. That's how you play baseball. When you're a professional like Albert is, you don't glare out there. You don't throw your bat. You don't charge the mound. You just take the next pitch and hit into the seats."

I also got to call something that never had been done before or since. Cardinals third baseman Fernando Tatis hit two grand slams—off the same pitcher (Chan Ho Park of the Los Angeles Dodgers) in the same inning in the same game in Los Angeles in 1999. Why Park was still in the game for the second one I'll never know.

The people, especially presidents, I met over the years...I wouldn't trade those experiences for anything. I remember when President Bush was in St. Louis for the All-Star Game in 2009. There was a woman who came with him from the White House, and she wanted to go over what I could ask and not ask. I said, "I'm going to ask him about the [Gulf] War."

Horrified, she said, "Oh, no! You can't do that."

I didn't, but she got all nervous. I knew his late uncle, Bucky Bush, real well. I used to play golf with him, and he was in the background that day laughing. And when Bush's dad was also president, Bucky called and said the president was coming to the game. We were in L.A. at the time. So I was just standing there with the two trainers, and the president walked into the clubhouse and said, "Hey, Mike, how ya doin?'"

For many years, I would alternate between radio and television when we had a TV game. But baseball is made for radio—not that people don't watch it on TV. There's about a 10-second delay from radio so they'll watch TV but not until they listen to it on radio and those 10 seconds are up. They'll listen to the game and they'll look at it when there's a home run or something.

The audience is the most important thing. It's not me or John Rooney, my last broadcast partner; it's the broadcast. And I've always treated it like that. The biggest compliment I get is when a visually impaired person brings his radio to the game and listens to it while he or she's there. They can tell what's going on. You know you're doing your job when a guy, who can't really see, can see what's going on. You have to paint the picture on radio for that fan.

Another test was in the bullpen in Kansas City. They could get the game on KMOX there so they'd listen to the

St. Louis broadcast in the bullpen. They would know if you were doing it right.

Football is made for television, but not baseball. For instance, Caray might have embellished things a little when there wasn't much baseball on TV, but he had those folks in Potosi, Missouri, on the edge of their seats on every pitch. You might not have been watching the same game, but you were on the edge of your seat. I didn't realize how important the job was until people were telling me, "Don't retire." Now that they know I've retired, they kind of take it for granted. But it's not going to be easy for the next guy.

I didn't do much statistical analysis when I broadcast. I didn't have all the stats that other announcers had. But I didn't need them. I just told the people what the hell's going on or what I thought was going on. That's where Rooney came in. I could ask him, "How many doubles or triples does this guy have?" And he had it right there. He came to the ballpark as well-prepared as anybody I've ever worked with. He puts it all in his computer. He takes about an hour and a half to put it in there. If he doesn't get it in there, he doesn't feel whole for the game. I couldn't ask Jack the same stat I might be looking for from Rooney because Jack didn't have any idea. That wasn't the way he operated, and I would never ask a question of a person on the air that I knew he wouldn't have the answer for.

The unsung heroes of these broadcasts are the producer/engineers we've had, and there basically have been only three of them in my time—Tom Barton, Colin Jarrett, and Jim Jackson. Jackson is still doing it. They are tremendously important, the most important basically. And when Rooney came here, I told him that there was one guy that was important here, and that was Jackson.

One of the things you have to learn is how to fill the air on radio. You can tell when there's dead air and you need to say something right away. That's one of the easier parts. On TV you can have dead air. When I wasn't working games—when I had my time off in the later years—I would still listen to the games. I would have the TV on if I needed to see something. A lot of times, there was that 10-second difference.

Television is basically easier. And I think most great TV guys came from radio, like Vin Scully, for instance. Scully, the Dodgers' great broadcaster, said he wasn't going to vote for anybody until I got in the Hall of Fame. To me, that's the ultimate compliment because I think Scully's a bell ringer. I don't think I'm alone either. Before one of the playoffs we had with the Dodgers, he called me and asked if his wife could sit in my booth. I said, "Sure." She apparently had a bad experience sitting in the stands a few years before that.

Baseball is made for the daytime. If you turned to all night games, which I can understand because you're following the money, you would kill it.

Not much has surprised me on the field because I went through it all as a player, though the first Saturday game I did on television for NBC was a weird one. The producer and director told the lead broadcaster that it was my first game, so to be careful. Anyway, he never called on me until there was a play he didn't understand and then he just turned and looked at me.

Something had happened, like a fight on the field. I jumped in and explained it, and he got up and left and told the producer, "Give it to him. Let him do it."

For most of my career, I did every game—162 of them. People ask me about how many games did I do total? I don't know. But I do know that every game is different. That's one of the great charms about it. Every time you go to the ballpark, you don't know what's going to happen. It could be a no-hitter. It could be a perfect game. Somebody could hit four home runs. I've seen the no-hitters by one pitcher and four home runs by one hitter.

Mark Whiten hit four home runs in the second game of a twi-night doubleheader at Cincinnati. I covered Bob Forsch's two no-hitters. But when Lou Brock broke the stolen-base record, I just got up and left because I figured it was Jack's call. Calling those things are about as much fun as experiencing them as a player.

For much of the time, though, games weren't on TV a lot, so the radio calls were even more important. Now, every one of the games is on TV. But with the pandemic, I could see regional telecasters instead of a guy traveling to see just one team. The games will come to them instead of them going to the games if you know what I mean. Like for St. Louis, regional games would be Kansas City, St. Louis, Cincinnati, Chicago, and places like that.

One of my favorites with whom to work on television was Jay Randolph, a former pro golfer who had won the Egyptian Open and had the confidences of Jack and Barbara Nicklaus, Arnold Palmer, and many in the golf community. He also knew every golf course and the fastest way to get there. We were going to play golf in Philadelphia one day, and Randolph and I were out the night before, and he had two bottles of wine. So the next day, I told my friend, "You and I are going to play his best ball."

He said, "What are you doing? We can't beat him."

I said, "Trust me."

So Randolph beat the snot out of us over the first nine holes. And then I pressed him. My friend again said, "What the hell are you doing?

Again, I said, "Trust me. I know he can drink one bottle of wine, but he can't drink two."

We beat the tar out of him on the second nine.

I've been nominated for the Hall of Fame's broadcasting award a couple of times, but I didn't make it. I don't know if it would mean a lot to me. It means more on the financial side. And it means a lot more to your family than it does to you. It has a nice ring, let's put it that way.

But the ultimate is the ballplayers who are in the Hall of Fame. A great advantage I had for my job was that I played. I remember a guy asking me, "What makes you so sure you know what you're talking about?"

I said, "I can watch a brain operation a thousand times. But who do you want to do the operation? Me? Or the surgeons?"

I do take pride in knowing so many people in the game that I wouldn't have any trouble getting a five-minute interview from anybody. That was because I was fair, and they trusted me. Plus, the fact I was going to ask intelligent questions. The writers ask stupid questions sometimes. But it's just normal. I'm ignorant when it comes to certain things. You have the points you're interested in. And what you're not interested in, you don't give a damn about.

I was interested in baseball and I wasn't interested in crossword puzzles or things like that.

I probably wouldn't have been as good in my job if I'd been somewhere else. But in the last couple of years, I couldn't go down and talk to the manager—when that was taken away from me because of COVID-19. I'm a hard-headed guy. I didn't go down there anymore.

You can see that attendance was well down from what they expected, and the average fan isn't stupid. He's so tired of seeing the players do what they're doing. They get disgruntled. The owners want to have the designated hitter this year, and now there's fewer decisions for the managers to make—and for the fans to make. They like to manage, too. Now, with the DH, they're going to take that away from the fans. In the long run, I think that's going to hurt the game.

I've found that players just want to respect a manager. They don't care if they like him or not. A manager does have to understand the game better if he wasn't a great player who can rely on his experiences there. I did know the game and I take credit for some of these fans knowing what's going on because I taught them over the radio.

One of the things I would concentrate on as a manager was defense. People worry so much about offense, but you can affect a game much more defensively than you can offensively, especially if you're an infielder because you know you're going to bat only three or four times. You might have a half dozen or more times a game you can impact the game as an infielder.

They're trying to shorten the games now, but all they're doing is making them longer. We see more arguments with hitters on strike calls than we ever have. They're all "due" hitters. If the ball is a few inches outside, they won't swing at it. They've got to have their pitch to swing at. But when the game evolves, the strike zone changes with it. Who runs the game? The owners? No, the umpires. If they wanted to speed up the game, all they've got to do is call strikes in those games, and it would be a much more exciting game. We don't need all the changes that baseball is trying to make.

How do we operate now with the smart phones when we didn't have the smart phones 10 years ago, 20 years ago? Why don't I have a smart phone? Because I don't need one. My wife has two of them. My broadcast partners and engineer have two of them, so why do I need one? I'll need one now that I'm retired. If I want to see what show's playing at the theater, that's the easiest way to find out. Or if I want to find a restaurant that's open. But I will say that I was going to meet a friend of mine for breakfast at 9:00 one day in 2020, and when we got there, the restaurant was closed. If I had had a smart phone, I would have known that. So I guess I outsmarted myself.

JOE BUCK

To do anything for 50 years is remarkable. But to think of where Mike Shannon started in '72—I was three years old then, and he was kind of coming over for Broadcasting 101 lessons—to have that impact and to have that comforting feeling that his voice brings, it not only comes with longevity, but it also comes with somebody who can entertain and educate.

I say all the time that his impact to St. Louis Cardinals fans and their understanding of the game and the way the game works—what managers are looking for, what scouts are looking for, and really every phase of the game—was a master's class for me as a kid being in that booth, hearing about the game, and being around somebody who played in the glory days of Major League Baseball in the 1960s. Hearing about the guys he played with and against, it was like he was a walking encyclopedia of knowledge as far as what made certain players great and who had the biggest impact on him and why.

I owe as much to Mike personally for my understanding of baseball as I do my dad or anybody else. My dad is No. 1, but Mike is 1A to me.

But I'm no different than any other Cardinals fan because if they were paying attention, they got the same knowledge that I got by sitting there and listening. As I said at his roast a few years ago, I just can't imagine what that was like for him to work with me. He could have shut that down right away even before I started doing games at 21 years old. The minute I had a real conversation with him on air about baseball and strategy— whatever was going on with the Cardinals at the time—gave me instant credibility that I could hold my own. That's kind of what I sensed with Tim

McCarver a few years later on national TV. He could have fought that. But I had as much fun with Mike on the road as anybody I've ever traveled with. I learned a lot about life and just how the world works from being around him. I learned so much from him, and just one-tenth of it is baseball. I've said this a million times. I don't know what the definition of "street smart" is but that's him. He is just a guy that has a unique way of looking at life and situations.

To grow up in that environment and go from sitting with his son, Danny, at the kids' table to being one of the broadcasters and to wind up at that strip joint, Wanda's, in Montreal on the day of my first game as I was filling in for my dad was something. I was sitting there with him and Red Schoendienst and C.J. Cherre, our traveling secretary, and Cliff Day, the TWA flight rep, and then we went to Olympic Stadium. What a way for your first day to happen.

I'm sure that was all coordinated by Mike.

But the most important thing is that Mike loves Cardinals baseball. And when he said one day during the season, "This team's not very good," that carries tremendous weight. I see a lot of the same things around him that I saw from my dad, which was getting strength and life from being around those players and the team.

What people don't understand is how funny he is and how quick-witted he is. I've been on the bus with him and on the charter with him, and he can hold court the way they talk about Bob Uecker, the great Milwaukee Brewers broadcaster. There would be times when Mike would be in the front row of the bus, and he would have the entire attention of everybody on the bus and be cracking up everybody whether he was talking about Schoendienst or whoever.

I just think he's "whip smart" in his own way, and that blends into his sense of humor. He's devoted his life to telling people about Cardinals baseball, and around that he's carved out one of the most unique existences of anybody—whether it's landing in the middle of the night after a charter flight, taking a nap, and then going to fish at 5:00 in the morning or going to play golf all day and then rolling into the ballpark. He's squeezed every drop of life of every chance he's made for himself. He's the least lazy person I've ever been around.

I guess he's become sort of famous for some of the things he said that didn't seem to make much sense at the time, but they all had their own logic. They all have the Mike Shannon logic behind them. I know a lot of people must have been thinking, *Oh, my God, he must have been drinking all day or all night* when he said something curious. But I can tell you I never saw him drink in the broadcast booth. And he didn't. That's just him. That's what people don't get.

So when you have the quote-unquote "Shannonisms," those are not "Shannonisms" because he's been drinking whiskey sours all day. Those are "Shannonisms" because that's what his brain came up with. And they have all their own footing in logic, and even if you call him on it, he can kind of wiggle his way out of whatever situation he put himself in by saying something kind of different. And you walk away shrugging your shoulders and saying, "I guess that makes sense."

I was there for a lot of them like when we got a note that 200 French foreign exchange students were in the ballpark that day. He said, "I wonder where they're from, Joe."

And I said, "France?"

And he said, "Yeah, if you can speak French, you can speak any language. It's not like Chinese, which has a bunch of different derelicts."

I said, "You mean dialects."

And he said, "Yeah, but they've got a lot of derelicts there, too."

He can save any situation at the end with that little cackle that he had. When he does it, it just makes you smile. You think about it. You scratch your head. And you move on.

But he should have won the Frick Broadcast Award and been in the Hall of Fame wing for broadcasters by now. Maybe some of that is that he wasn't the play-by-play man all the time he did Cardinals games. Honestly, I don't know the entire list of who votes, who doesn't, and why they vote the way they do. Yes, for a long time, he was considered the analyst, but as many of us who sat there in that booth and worked those games know, there really is no "analyst," per se. If you're not doing play-by-play, you're basically doing color analysis right next to the person who is. I did it. You're just there to support the other guy. He's definitely the lead. He's been the lead forever. It all wheels off Mike. There's no two ways about that.

When he's not there…that will be just a major hole that will never be filled entirely. I like to think that applied to my dad. But it's the same way about Mike. They've used that position of being that radio voice of the team to do good for others. I'm talking about raising money as Mike has done forever and how my dad did for various charities. It comes with a huge responsibility, and that means giving back in the community.

It's still the No. 1 job in radio. He's been there since 1972. And if you're there for that long—50 years—you're in the No. 1 position on the No. 1 radio network. That should speak for itself.

In a word, he's beloved. You hear his voice and immediately you are comforted. That's how I felt when I was away at camp, and somebody had the Cardinals game on, or if I was driving back from college at the University of Indiana. The minute you pick up that radio signal…all is well. It's like a comfortable sweater. You put it on—and relax.

It's 50 years later now, but Mike remembers everything. I had the pleasure of knowing him as a kid and now knowing him just as a broadcast contemporary. But I also did that *Live at Shannon's* show on Friday and Saturday and I had more fun doing that than any job I've ever had in broadcasting. It was a who's who of whoever was coming through town. They came over there to eat good food and just to hang out with Mike and reminisce about the game on the radio. That was as good of an education as any young broadcaster could have, which I got to do for years. I'm not sure that show could exist in 2021 from its past form with some of the things that were said and done there. You just never knew what Mike was going to come up with. The microphones just happened to be there.

CHAPTER 6

Hall of Fame Managers

For much of my career, I've had the privilege of broadcasting St. Louis Cardinals games managed by four Hall of Fame managers. I also played with and for Red Schoendienst, one of the four. And I played with Joe Torre, too. And then were the other Hall of Famers: Whitey Herzog and Tony La Russa. All those managers were easy to deal with. Their philosophies were pretty much the same in one regard, at least. As long as you showed up on time and you were better than the next guy, they let you play.

I played for Schoendienst most of my career, and both from that vantage point and from the booth, I can tell you he was a lot smarter than people thought he was. He was as good as anybody I've ever seen at picking talent. But like most managers, he got fired. Schoendienst was a man of few words, but when he spoke, you listened and you had to kind of pick out what you wanted. Schoendienst wasn't going to help you. If you needed more, you were going to have to find it yourself. He wasn't like Herzog.

Herzog enjoyed the whole process, especially dealing with the media. He made it easier for you. They were all different, and you just had to figure it out. But that's all part of the job.

Jack Buck and I would play cutthroat pinochle with Herzog all the time on the team charter planes. Herzog had a great advantage because he had a photographic memory, and that's pretty important when it comes to pinochle. He was a lot better than we were, let's put it that way.

Herzog really took advantage of Buck, who was not a very good player but thought he was. If I had a photographic memory, I would have been pretty good in that game, too. You would ask Herzog about a particular hit that a guy got, and he would say, "Right before that, he hit a foul ball down the left-field line." How could he remember that stuff? He's amazing.

But one of the things he was really good at was forgetting about a loss about as soon as it happened. To be a manager, you have to be hard-boiled because what ticks you off may not tick off the next guy. You have to determine what's good and what's bad, and sometimes it's not easy. Really, a manager is only as good as his players. The guy the Cardinals had the last few years, Mike Shildt, handled the bullpen better than anybody I've seen. You don't know how good he'd be with a good team because he's never had a really good team. He's made teams better than they are. I don't know how he did it. But he never had a losing season, just like his predecessor, Mike Matheny, who was here five-and-a-half seasons compared to three and a half for Shildt. They had one thing in common. They didn't win the World Series, though Matheny got to one in 2013. And they both got fired.

As the years go on, you get to know a manager and how he handles a game because of his tendencies. That's part of your job to follow along and be ready to present that to the listeners when they ask, "What's he doing here?" Sometimes, these guys are uncanny, and that's why they've got the job, I guess.

You can learn a lot about managers in spring training. Herzog used to have these guys he called his "cocktail pitchers," meaning that when it was time for the manager and the writers and broadcasters to go have cocktails after a game—they were all day games then—he would put in a pitcher in the ninth inning that he knew was going to give up a home run or at least the winning run. A pitcher came up to him one day and said, "Whitey, I really appreciate you taking me on all these trips." Little did he know.

The good managers know how to lose when it doesn't count. And if they're going to lose, they're going to lose in a hurry. Herzog never took his job too seriously at that time of the year. There was one particular game in Clearwater,

Florida, where the Cardinals and Philadelphia Phillies were tied in the bottom of the ninth. The player we just mentioned was pitching and allowed a one-out triple in the ninth. Herzog had this figured out. He ordered the next two hitters walked intentionally. In theory, he was setting up a force-out at every base or even hoping for a double play. But nobody walks anybody intentionally in spring games. Nobody.

Sure enough, the count went to 3–0, and the equipment manager, Buddy Bates, already was gathering up the bats and other game materials from the dugout and starting to head down the third-base line to where the bus was parked that was taking the Cardinals back to their spring training headquarters in St. Petersburg. And sure enough, the pitcher threw ball four, the winning run trotted home, and it was time for cocktails.

Then there are other managers who thought they were smart and had the game figured out. That scared the hell out of me because this game is hard to figure out. This game will bite you in the butt. But Herzog knew when he was outgunned. He would say, "I've got this little cap pistol, and the other guy's got a cannon."

I think he enjoyed getting his butt beat once in a while, and he had some of his best quotes after his team had been hammered. But he always had an angle. When he knew he was outgunned, he didn't fight it. Most guys wouldn't admit that. He threw up a white flag and saved it for another day. He would lose a game 14–2 and say, "It's a good thing it only counted as one [loss]."

I know there were many, many times Herzog sent a guy up there to hit, knowing he was going to make an out. But he had to do it to save somebody else. He knew he had to do it.

Sometimes you can't see the forest for the trees. Sometimes you're just outgunned. Herzog would say, "I don't want to play the 10th inning. I'd rather win or lose in the ninth."

Herzog did a lot more winning than losing as the record will show. Not only did he manage the Cardinals to three National League pennants and one World Series title from 1982 to 1987, but he also won three consecutive division championships in 1976–78 when he was with the Kansas City Royals, who ran into the New York Yankees every time in the championship series and lost—once in four games and the other two times in five games. If Herzog hadn't lost Jack Clark to an ankle injury late in 1987 and Vince Coleman, the stolen base king who was swallowed up by the "Killer Tarp," in 1985, he would have had two more World Series titles in St. Louis in addition to the one he won in 1982 against the Milwaukee Brewers.

The 1985 loss for Herzog did bother him more than most others because he felt his team was robbed when it had a 1–0 lead in Game Six, needing only three more outs to win the World Series. But first-base umpire Don Denkinger made a horrendous call at the bag, ruling that Jorge Orta had beaten reliever Todd Worrell, who had taken first baseman Clark's throw. It wasn't even close as Worrell will forever know because he put a photograph of the play in his den. But there was no instant replay then. Herzog knew he was outgunned the next night before Game Seven—at least emotionally. "We had it taken away from us last night," he said privately. "We haven't got a chance."

He was correct. With Bret Saberhagen needing little help, the Royals beat the Cardinals 11–0 to win Game Seven and the World Series. When the score had reached 10–0 about halfway through the game, Herzog brought in temperamental righthander Joaquin Andujar to pitch, knowing fully well that Andujar and Denkinger, now doing home plate, would get into it about balls and strikes as Andujar had in Game Three with another American League umpire. (They had separate umpires for each league then.) Andujar did get into it with Denkinger, and both he and Herzog got tossed.

If there was a category for best manager/general manager, Herzog would win easily.

Herzog had taken over a bad Cardinals team in June of 1980 from Kenny Boyer. He ascended to general manager in September that year, and Schoendienst took over for the final month as manager as the Cardinals limped home with a 74–88 record. Herzog promised a search for a new manager and an overhaul. He hired himself back as manager and in five days in December shuffled the deck.

First, he signed catcher Darrell Porter as a free agent from Kansas City. That meant that incumbent catcher Ted Simmons would move to first base, and incumbent first baseman Keith Hernandez, the league co-MVP the year before, would move to left field. That would happen for the first six innings of the game, and then Hernandez would wind up at first base with Simmons perhaps out of the game. At first, Simmons, the Cardinals' top offensive threat, said he was okay with this, but he changed his mind the more he thought about it.

Pitching, especially relief pitching, was one of the Cardinals' weak spots. So on Sunday night before the winter meetings officially began in 1980, Herzog swung an 11-player deal with the San Diego Padres, bringing pitcher Bob Shirley, catcher Gene Tenace, and, most importantly, premier closer Rollie Fingers to the Cardinals. In return Herzog gave up prized catcher Terry Kennedy and six spare parts, which Herzog made San Diego general manager Jack McKeon take in order to get Kennedy. Bullish on relievers, Herzog went after Chicago Cubs ace Bruce Sutter the next day. He dealt first baseman Leon Durham and third baseman Ken Reitz, who had to be bought out of a no-trade clause, to get Sutter. And then they went from having no closer to having two future Hall of Fame closers.

Herzog thought he should call and ask both Fingers and Sutter if they could co-exist. One would have to pitch the eighth inning in a set-up role once in a while when the other had the ninth. Sutter said he could do that. Fingers had some reservations, so Herzog then considered moving Fingers. About this time, Simmons decided he didn't want to have to move to an unfamiliar position at first base. Simmons had a no-trade provision but would waive it under the right circumstances. Herzog, still seeking starting pitching help, took a shot at getting Ron Guidry from the Yankees or making a deal with Milwaukee to get Lary Sorensen and Dave LaPoint plus outfielder Sixto Lezcano and outfielder David Green, the Brewers' top prospect.

The Milwaukee deal was agreed upon. Simmons took a buyout, and the deal was done on Thursday. The Cards had an almost completely new deck. On Friday Herzog came to the press room at Loew's Anatole Hotel in Dallas and apologized to the media. "Boys," he said, "I haven't gotten anything for you today. Sorry."

La Russa later became a front-office type, though never at the same time as manager. He had a totally different philosophy of managing than Herzog. The first game of spring training was the biggest game he ever managed. I said, "What the hell?"

But he was right in his thinking, and it took me a while to get used to that. He wanted his team to play the first game of spring training like it was the seventh game of the World Series, and it never made any sense to me until I figured out his philosophy. He was serious about that stuff. La Russa was especially serious about he used his bullpen and he always wanted to have a lights-out closer, which is the way most managers operate today. If you don't have a closer, you have no chance in today's game. You could do it by committee, but you've got to be a smart SOB.

I didn't agree with a lot of La Russa's strategy. But you can't argue with his success, and I said it on the air. I didn't realize that he used to run the TV and radio feeds back every day after the games and learn stuff by doing that. He said to me one day that somebody had asked me about execution, and that I had said, "Yeah, it's very important. Unless you're on Death Row. Then it's not so damn important."

La Russa liked that line a lot. He's still quoting that line 20 years later and he even gives me credit for it. La Russa's record speaks for itself, too. In 16 seasons with the Cardinals, he got them into three World Series, winning two, including in 2011 after which he said he was retiring, which I really didn't believe. The Cardinals played in seven National League Championship Series under him. But he was at his best in the division series. The Cardinals always came out of the blocks fast in the postseason. In the nine division series he managed for the Cardinals, they lost only two of them, and La Russa's division series won-lost record in those 16 years was an amazing 23–10. And you know what he did with the Oakland A's, winning one World Series and playing in two others from 1988 to 1990. And with the Chicago White Sox, he won division titles unbelievably nearly 40 years apart—in 1983 and 2021.

Joe Torre didn't win any division series or any titles when he was with the Cardinals. But he would have been in postseason play if he had any pitching. You give him pitching and an owner who spends money like George Steinbrenner and combine that with Torre's ability as a native New Yorker to work and survive in that New York environment, just look at the results: four World Series titles with the Yankees in a five-season span from 1996 to 2000.

Schoendienst managed 12 full seasons with the Cardinals and, while the last eight years weren't all that productive, he had two great World Series teams that I played on in 1967–68.

Who's to say what's right and what's wrong? I'll tell you one thing, though. When a guy says he knows everything about the game, I get as far away from him as I can. But none of these guys said that. Schoendienst didn't tell you what he knew. But he knew it all, and everybody knew him. One day after a game in Japan when we were playing an exhibition series after the 1968 season was over, we went to dinner and we're walking back to the hotel, and somebody sees him on the street and says, "Red Schoendienst! Red Schoendienst!"

I said, "I can't take you anywhere, can I?"

I was just an average big leaguer after being a three-sport high school star in St. Louis. But I wish La Russa was there when I was a player. I wish I had played for him because he makes his players so much better. He never threw any of them under the bus. Herzog was smart like that, too. Sometimes, if you are an ex-player, you look at a manager and wonder, *What would he have done with me?*

But one thing about La Russa that I could never understand is why he wouldn't make the opposing closer work harder by having his hitters take some pitches during a late-inning at-bat. He told me that when he was a rookie he was a horse manure hitter like I was, and they gave him the take sign. He said he wouldn't tell any of his players to do that. Actually, La Russa was far worse than I was a hitter. While he was an outstanding minor league hitter, La Russa batted just .199 in the big leagues with no homers. I hit .255 with 68 homers.

La Russa and Schoendienst didn't give away their secrets very easily. And they didn't give them away to people who didn't understand them. When La Russa was the manager, he talked to Schoendienst almost every day. Why wouldn't you? Schoendienst wasn't an official coach then, but he was there every day in spring training and on the field before all the regular-season games until he would go upstairs to watch in the press box.

I never criticize a manager. I'll tell you about the options he has. But I've never pushed the buttons. Until you've been down there and have gotten to push the buttons, that's a tough job.

As a former player, I can tell you why a player made a mistake or why he made an error because he looked up and took his eye off the ball or whatever. That's because I made all those mistakes. I can relate and I can tell people what's going through a player's mind—or not going through his mind on a particular play. Instead of being totally critical, I would talk about what might have gone right on a particular play. You don't have to say, "How could he possibly do that?" Those fans, who are listening or watching, are smart enough to know that. You can tell them a little bit of the why. But I can't relate as a manager.

When Schoendienst was 95 and dying a few years ago, he was with a bunch of kids in their 30s and said, "I feel sorry for you guys."

They said, "What do you mean?"

He said, "I feel sorry for you because you didn't have the experiences that I had."

He went through the Depression, the wars, the whole ball of wax.

What a time we had in St. Louis, starting with him. From 1965 to 2011, almost 50 years, we basically had four managers—Red, Whitey, Joe, Tony. They were all known by their first names. All of them were different. All of them were winners. La Russa and Herzog won World Series while I was broadcasting. I had La Russa for 16 years and Herzog for 10, so I know more about La Russa. And La Russa broke Schoendienst's record for wins as a Cardinals manager.

Herzog was one of the best I ever saw at knowing how to relax after a game. He knew how to get away, which is sometimes hard for a guy. It was very hard for La Russa sometimes.

Herzog knew all the answers. Basically, that was it. You could never stump that son of a gun.

I'm sure that smart writers ask questions where they want to be stumped because they don't know the answer. It's the same with my job when I'm talking to a manager. People don't want to know what I say about something. They want to know what the manager says. When I would ask Herzog about his team, he would start with the closer. I thought he would start with the starting pitching. He managed the game backward. That's when I said, "Wow! I don't know what I'm doing. He's a lot smarter than I am when it comes to managing."

And then when he stepped up to become general manager and he was looking for a new manager after the 1980 season, he said, "What am I looking at when it's right in front of me?"

And that was when he hired himself back as manager.

I always figured La Russa would come back as a manager, but the only guy smart enough to hire him, White Sox owner Jerry Reinsdorf, was the one who hired him—and fired him—before. Reinsdorf pulled the wool over everybody's eyes on that one. I've got to give Reinsdorf credit because he wants to win, and he didn't care what the media said, and most of them didn't give Reinsdorf very high marks for hiring a 76-year-old and giving him a three-year contract.

The writers were still criticizing him when La Russa had that White Sox team out front by 10 ½ games.

A lot of owners don't care about winning. They just care about the money. Could I have made it 50 years in broadcasting with any other team? I never really thought

At the age of 10, I hang out with my siblings. (Courtesy Shannon family)

Gary Kolb (left) and I sit next to the great Stan Musial during his final season in 1963.

I round third base after hitting a two-run homer in the sixth inning of Game One of the 1964 World Series.

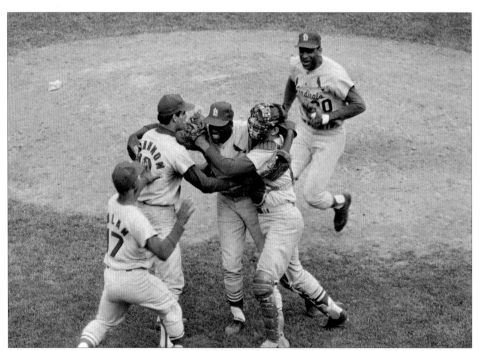

Tim McCarver and I embrace Bob Gibson following his complete-game, three-hitter to win Game Seven of the 1967 World Series.

My good buddy, Roger Maris, and I do calisthenics drills during the first day of spring training in 1968.

Outfielder Vada Pinson, Roger Maris' replacement, and I have fun with Maris in spring training of 1969, which was the year after Maris had retired.

I hoist my grandson, Maddoc, after throwing out the first pitch for the last regular-season game at Busch Stadium II in 2005.

I'm surrounded by two great former Cardinals players, Joe Torre (left) and Red Schoendienst, in spring training of 2008.

I announce a game against the Houston Astros with my great and longtime partner, John Rooney, in September of 2010.

I kiss my wife, Lori, during my 70th birthday celebration in 2009.

Fourth from the left, I get inducted into the Cardinals Hall of Fame with other Cardinals greats, including Jim Edmonds and Willie McGee, in 2014.

I acknowledge the best fans in baseball prior to our 2018 home opener.

I salute the home crowd during one of my final broadcasts on August 25, 2021.

During my final regular-season game on October 3, 2021 after 50 years as Cardinals broadcaster, I speak during a farewell ceremony, which the Cardinals thoughtfully organized.

about that. You have to be in the right place at the right time. But all I know is that most of the time I've been here, the Cardinals have had really good teams. I expected that because they had a winning attitude in the organization. Some of these other teams never seemed to understand what it took to win. Pitching and defense are what wins. Yet, some of these other teams go for offense. It doesn't make sense.

On some of our teams we'd create something out of nothing. Lou Brock would walk, steal second, go to third on a ground-out, and score on a sacrifice fly. We'd go ahead 1–0 and we wouldn't have even had a hit yet. Late in my final season with the Cardinals, I said something to the effect that, "This is a horse(bleep) team." The only difference was that everybody else was horse(bleep), too. What we were watching was unbelievable when you think about it.

This all went south when the owners started paying guys for the wrong reasons. They'd never played the game so they don't know. Like when we had the rule where you put a guy on second base with nobody out in the 10th inning. Ninety percent of the time he was scoring, right? Why don't teams play it like that—moving the runner over—the whole game? I'll tell you why. Because they don't pay the players for it. It doesn't matter if you strike out anymore. You can't make chicken salad out of chicken feathers, I guess. I see stuff nowadays…I just shake my head. On the other hand, the owners have exactly what they wanted.

You go back to those 1980s Cardinals teams under Herzog. They pushed it big time on the bases, and that was a very exciting team as they stole 300 bases. The whole league doesn't steal many more than that now. For Herzog, it must have been a lot of fun. That's a question I would have liked to have asked him—was it more fun to manage that team rather than a team that didn't have the talent to do that? It's an obvious answer, but that's important in your job and mine. It's about how you ask the question. And when.

These fans are good fans here. They understand the game, and I think I had a lot to do with that by trying to analyze the game and give them all the options a manager has—because he's got like four or five options on every play. Which one is he going to take? But the options aren't as many these days because you rarely see the bunt anymore, especially from a position player. I knew things were messed up when the people who run the game said that RBIs don't count. In my mind, there are only three things that count—scoring runs, driving in runs, and preventing runs. What determines who wins and loses? Runs, right? It doesn't take a genius to figure that out.

As a broadcaster, you have to treat a really good player differently. When Mark McGwire was the whole show, you had to figure out how to treat him. If there was a guy who deserved equal time for a Star of the Game show after a game, you had to pick him over Big Mac. Sometimes, you pick the lesser guy on purpose because you knew he wasn't going to be in there the next day. But Big Mac was hitting all those home runs; it was pretty hard not to pick him.

TONY LA RUSSA

Mike Shannon has that important credential that he was in uniform. He was a player, so he experienced that along with two world championships. And he stayed close to the team as a broadcaster, like Red Schoendienst stayed close to the team as a coach. Mike not only experienced the greatness of being a player there in St. Louis, but then he also got to be the guy who people would tune in to and rely on.

I don't want to disrespect others who did not play in the big leagues—and even Jack Buck. There is a reality in the booth as to how difficult that game is down there. I'm not sure you can really appreciate how hard it is to catch a routine ball and throw it accurately. Or take an at-bat or make a pitch against the best in the world. Having those experiences really helped define the way he broadcast games. Plus, his personality. There's so much to his life, and he's such a fun guy. I tell a lot of our guys about the line Mike has when talking about how the game should be played right and the importance of execution. And Mike would say that the only people who would disagree on the importance of execution are the guys on death row. That's hilarious.

GET UP, BABY!

I became friends with Mike that first year I was there in 1996. There were a lot of questions about whether somebody from the American League, where I had been with the Oakland A's and Chicago White Sox, could manage the St. Louis Cardinals. On one of those first road trips— we were going to San Diego—he walks up to me on the plane and says, "Hey, big boy, what are you doing when we land?"

I said that I didn't have any plans. So he said, "Where are you and I going to dinner?"

That dinner was all about understanding the responsibility everybody in that uniform had to keep the legacy alive and play the game the right way. While we were around, it was up to the coaching staff and me to maintain that legacy. That dinner and what he said were very impactful.

I knew about the Cardinals. I'd come as a fan to the 1982, 1985, and 1987 World Series in St. Louis when I was managing in the American League. When I came to those World Series and walked around, I could feel the excitement of the fans. The other thing was that I was born in Tampa, Florida, and on Sunday, the only day my dad didn't work, we'd either go to Tampa to watch the White Sox or the Cincinnati Reds in spring training or we'd drive across the bridge and watch the New York Yankees and the Cardinals in St. Petersburg. So I was seeped into the lore of the game from Day One, and the Cardinals were part of that lore.

As the years went along for me in St. Louis, I would spend hundreds of nights on the road with Mike, whether we were having dinner after a game or just talking ball. When I think of Mike, I think of his stamina, so those could turn into some long nights. Finally, I would go to bed, and three or four hours later, he'd get up and go out to fish. I didn't do that, couldn't do that. I had enough trouble just making out a lineup.

When he's not broadcasting in 2022—there are so many memories people have of him and those memories are so strong. It's the same as with Jack Buck. Fans have listened to Mike every day for 50 years.

As he has said, Mike never pushed the buttons as a manager, but he was so good at presenting the alternatives in any situation. There's always some stuff that's going on down there. I had that experience when I wasn't managing with the Arizona Diamondbacks, the Los Angeles Angels, and Boston Red Sox; I was in the front office instead. To the people upstairs, the answers seem so obvious, but it's not obvious. There are things that can happen inning to inning, and you get information about how it feels, doesn't feel, or what you're seeing, and Mike was exactly right.

I go back to the word "stamina" with Mike. Fifty years in broadcasting. Beyond that, he had to have a very unique gift—or a talent. There's no way he would have lasted that long unless fans appreciated and enjoyed what he had to say.

The Cardinals really stressed playing the game hard and playing the game right, making the fewest mistakes. When you talk about execution, it's in all phases: pitchers making pitches, base running, defensive plays, good at-bats. And he understood that. He's a very smart guy. His insights were helpful. I've been mentored by the best of them—Mike as well. I was very, very fortunate to spend those 16 years in St. Louis. I'll never be able to thank everyone enough.

CHAPTER 7

America's Guest and the Modern Game

One of the things I had to adapt to in my final couple of years was that I couldn't go downstairs to talk to the players and the manager. I could figure out stuff most times, but the manager liked it when I came down. But that was taken away from me because of the COVID-19 protocols, and after a while, I didn't want to go down there anyway. The game is different now, and the average fan can see it. These fans are so tired of seeing these players do what they're doing that they get disgruntled. And some of them have stopped going to games.

The owners are going to go add the designated hitter in the National League. But without the designated hitter and the pitcher hitting, the fan is allowed to make decisions, too. He gets to manage, and now they're going to take that away from him. When the pitcher did bat, what are you going to have him do? Does he bunt? Does he hit? And they're going to take that away, and that's going to hurt. But I didn't see pitchers trying to improve their bunting that much anyway.

They were getting $1 million a win. Why wouldn't they want to improve their bunting to give them a better chance to win when they're getting $1 million a win, and all they've got to do is bunt a guy over from first to second? That's why the owners were voting for the designated hitter. But they didn't think long enough.

Attendance is way down, right? Why? They've got better ballparks, but the average family's got four kids. So you're going to bring four kids to the game, and it's going to cost you $300 to $400, and you don't have $300 or $400. We got rained out one day at Busch Stadium this past season, and I was leaving at the same time the fans were and I ran into a guy who asked me how I was doing and I said, "Fine. How are you doing?"

He said, "Well, I bought 10 beers, and it cost me $100. My tickets cost $182, and I got rained out." So, for him it was a bad day.

It's an expensive proposition, so you'd better give the fans something to look at and enjoy. What's wrong with the way the game was being played? It didn't need to change.

Play smallball. Move a runner over when you make an out. You see the big guys always do that because the defense has to play deep. Players are rewarded when they hit a home run, but nothing is subtracted when they make an out that doesn't advance anybody. They don't have any stats for moving the runner over and they don't have any stats for running bases correctly or incorrectly.

The players today are in better shape, but they're not better players. They're better athletes and they're better trained. But how can you be better than Willie Mays, Hank Aaron, or a Stan Musial? Are the players stronger? Well, I'll say this: in the '40s, '50s, '60s, maybe five guys in the whole league could hit the ball out of the park to the opposite field. We've got 170-pound second basemen doing that now. So, something's different. I don't know what it is.

They have "launch angle" and all this crap. I knew it was bull when they said RBIs weren't that important. Who puts all this stuff into the computer, and then you're giving it to the coaches? That's what I want to know. There are only three things in the game that count: scoring runs, driving in runs, and preventing runs. What wins? Pitching and defense will always win, and they have for over 100 years. Good pitching will get out good hitting any day of the week, but people at the top level of baseball still go for offense rather than pitching. I don't understand it. There are so many examples of pitching winning pennants. And now managers keep changing pitchers every inning it seems. Do you suppose that a manager ever asks a pitcher any more to "give me one more out?"

While I'm waiting for my car to come up during the All-Star break in San Diego a long time ago, I ran into Ted

Williams, who was from San Diego and was there for some function. He said, "Mike, how come they're not swinging at a high pitch anymore?"

I said they weren't swinging at it because the umpires weren't calling it a strike anymore.

Then he wanted to ask me why hitters were wearing sunglasses. I got the manufacturing rep to send some to him. I told him, "Ted Williams needs some sunglasses." But when I was talking to him about them and why hitters were wearing them, I said, "That's going to take a little more time. We're going to have to sit down and talk about that."

The only time I really had a long meeting with Williams was the year I was in the front office in 1971 and went to the winter meetings. Williams—he was managing the Texas Rangers then—was talking hitting. Everybody else wound up leaving, but I stayed. I wanted to hear what he had to say. Damn, he was smart about hitting. He made an art out of it. At least, he thought it was an art. So he would have depicted it better than you or I would have depicted it. He looked more at the finer things of it than we would. I actually think his eyes slowed the ball down somehow.

If I was commissioner for a day, I would start all the games either at noon or midnight. I was always wide awake at midnight because I was always out and I saw the ball better at noon.

But I would sure expand the strike zone up. Tell the umpires to call the strike to where the letters are on the uniform jersey. That would speed up the game. People don't like the game today because there's no intrigue in it, you know? The good pitchers go inside and outside anyway. But up and down is easier as a hitter to adjust to unless the strike zone went up some more.

As far as some of the other new rules they had for the last couple of years, why do they only bunt or try to get a guy over from second in the 10th inning when the runner already is placed there? Why don't they play that way the rest of the game? Like in the second inning or the third inning or the fourth inning or the fifth inning? What's the difference? If you did something like that then, you wouldn't need the 10th inning at all. A bird in the hand is worth two in the bush, right? But let's at least wait another inning before you put a runner on base. Let's not do it until the 11th. Or put the best base runner you have at second base instead of the guy who made the last out the inning before. They're trying to shorten the game. That will speed it up. Who's making up the rules? Guys who have never played the game, right? You want to speed the game up? Change the strike zone or call it the way it's supposed to be called. Joe West would do that, but he's retiring.

West actually has a great line about me. He said that I have "a hard time putting any two or three sentences together without using profanity of some sort. However, he doesn't use profanity on the air when he's broadcasting."

He's right. I put this way: "I don't use profanity in church. And when I'm behind that microphone and talking to all these people, I assume I'm in the same state I'd be in if I was in church."

When I was first started broadcasting, they asked what I would do if I was a general manager, like my good friend and former teammate Dal Maxvill, who was with the St. Louis Cardinals. It was an easy answer for me. I said I would hire all the scouts who signed the Los Angeles Dodgers pitchers and all the scouts who signed all the San Francisco Giants hitters. Man, what a lineup the Giants used to have with Mays, Willie McCovey, Orlando Cepeda, Felipe Alou, Jim Ray Hart.

It will be interesting to see what the rules are for media this year as far as Zoom interviews and so forth. But I won't have to worry about that. I'll be listening to games, playing golf, and fishing. I could watch the games on TV, but I think baseball was made to be broadcast on the radio. When Red Schoendienst wasn't at the ballpark, he would have both the television and radio on, but he'd be walking around listening to the radio. When there was something he needed to see, he would go watch it on TV because there was about a 10-second delay. It was the best way of both worlds. He was definitely a very intelligent individual as far as knowing the game.

I'll still be involved as a Cardinals Hall of Famer. I'll be there on Opening Day and for the Hall of Fame ceremonies. But I told them the other day that they'd better limit those speeches when it's hot out there for the outdoor ceremonies in August. People still talk about trying to get me into the broadcast wing at the Hall of Fame in Cooperstown with the Ford C. Frick Award. I'm okay with not being in. But not much has happened lately in that regard. It's probably harder for me now, but maybe it would be easier for me if they had all the living candidates in one group and all the deceased in another group and vote that way.

When I got to 40 years in the booth, the club started a campaign to get me on the ballot, and it succeeded to a point. I did get on the ballot and I fully appreciated their support. I remember my broadcast partner, John Rooney, saying then, "It's Mike's time. Fifty-plus years with the organization, his 40th year in the booth, I think he's doing some of the best work of his career right now. He's at ease calling the game and he's having fun. Today, it's hard to get somebody in broadcasting who has your back." And then he added, "If you do, you're darn lucky. Too many people are looking to advance themselves. Mike is the ultimate team leader. He lets me do what I need to do."

Rooney kindly mentioned another thing he thought I brought to the table. He said, "You get guys in the booth, and they tell the same stories over and over. I'd think I'd heard it all, but with Mike, you hear something new all the time and you wonder, *Where's he getting those?*"

I've done a lot of things—playing, broadcasting, owning a restaurant—but the most fun for me was playing. That's your first love, and even when I was playing freshman football at Missouri, I was also playing outfield on the baseball team. I was pretty much only an outfielder then, though I pitched some in high school at Christian Brothers College. I pitched and batted fourth in high school.

There was some talk about making me a pitcher after I signed, but the Cardinals saw more of the potential I had as an everyday player. For some reason, that was more important for them. I had good speed, power, and a strong arm. I had no real interest in pitching anyway, not even one inning. I know Musial did that one time against the Chicago Cubs at the end of the season, but it wasn't for me. But if they had come to me and said, "We think you should become a pitcher full time," then I'd have better become a pitcher. They don't ask and they don't even suggest.

Sometimes in the major leagues, they'll have someone pitch an inning or two if a guy's getting his brains beat out. They'll bring in a position player. But they didn't do that in the minors. They would let a guy get his brains beat out because they would find out then that you had to make an adjustment. Unfortunately, pitchers don't have that ability now. Just look at the stats. They bring up a guy who was 2–22. They don't let them develop as they used to, but I guess the game is looked at differently than it was 40 or 50 years ago.

I played just the outfield positions, third base, and catcher in the majors. I didn't see any action at first base, second, or shortstop. Shortstop and catcher are positions you don't get an opportunity very much because they're specialized. However, there was a famous picture of me making a tag at second base. There were two umpires there making the call. One said, "Safe," and the other said, "Out," and the "Out" prevailed. John Kibler called out, and Ed Vargo called safe.

We were playing the Dodgers at home on May 12, 1969. Bill Sudakis hit a blooper to center field. Our shortstop, Steve Huntz, and second baseman Julian Javier both went out to chase the pop-up, and when center fielder Curt Flood picked up the ball, nobody was at second until I got there. Kibler had gone out into the outfield, but he got back to second to make the call, but Vargo didn't know if Kibler would get back or not. Kibler had recognized that Flood couldn't catch the ball before Flood did. Sudakis thought he had a double as he slid headfirst. Flood usually played deep, and Javier was usually able to catch those pop-ups. If Javier wasn't the second baseman, Flood couldn't have played so deep. I was the only guy who knew if the runner was out. One umpire was blocked by the slide, and the other one was behind the play. Neither one had a good view of it. Sudakis really was out. His hand was over the base, and I touched his hand. If he was fleet of foot, he would have made it. But he wasn't. The picture is hanging in my restaurant.

They tell me I'm only the 13th announcer in baseball history to serve as long as 50 years in the booth and only the sixth announcer to have at least 50 years with one team. Until I retired, I had the fourth longest active tenure among Major League Baseball announcers behind Jamie Jarrín (who started announcing the Dodgers in 1959), Denny Matthews (who started announcing the Kansas City Royals in 1969), and Bob Uecker (who started announcing the Milwaukee Brewers in 1971). When I was part of the Cardinals' television broadcasts, I received a local sports Emmy award for sports broadcasting in 1985. I was inducted into the Missouri Sports Hall of Fame in 1999 and was named Missouri Sportscaster of the Year in 2002, 2003, and 2014 by the National Sportscasters and Sportswriters Association.

I was inducted into the Cardinals Hall of Fame as part of the inaugural induction class in 2014 and was a finalist for the Frick Award in 2014 and 2020.

Besides playing in three World Series, I got to broadcast seven more with the Cardinals winning three of them, including the last one they won in 2011. That was the one David Freese tied in Game Six with a two-out triple in the ninth inning and won with a home run to lead off the 11th inning. The next time he batted, he doubled in two runs in the first inning of Game 7 to erase a Texas lead, and the Cardinals went on to a relatively easy 6–2 win. People will talk forever about how great Game Six was. But it was really the best—and worst—game you would ever see because both teams were making errors all over the place for much of the night, and a pop fly basically hit Freese on the head. Fans can remember it however they want, but that's how I will remember it—the worst (five total errors), which became the best. My call of Freese's home run went like this, according to the KMOX tape: "Swing and a high drive to center field. Get up, baby! Get up baby! Get up! Oh yeah! David Freese has just sent us into Game No. 7."

That series had some other great moments, though. How about Albert Pujols cracking three home runs—tying a record—to win the third game for the Cardinals? And much earlier that month, Chris Carpenter outpitched Philadelphia

Phillies ace Roy Halladay 1–0 in the fifth game of the division series as the first two Cardinals hitters of the game, Rafael Furcal and Skip Schumaker, hit a triple and a double, and that was the only scoring.

Freese long will be remembered as a hero, but he also struck out four out of five times during one stretch in the division series and almost was benched by Tony La Russa. After that dry spell, Freese went 23 for 50 with seven doubles, five home runs, and the infamous triple over the head of Nelson Cruz, who probably should have been playing deeper in right field because Freese hit so many balls to that part of the ballpark.

The 2006 World Series was the only one the Cardinals won in my time that didn't take seven games. We had a rookie, Anthony Reyes, who shocked the Tigers by beating them in Detroit in Game One. And the Tigers didn't recover. Their pitchers committed error after error, as if they hadn't taken any fielding practice or expected any bunts by the Cardinals. You know their manager, Jim Leyland, had prepared them for all that, but the message got lost somehow.

In 1982 the Cardinals won their first World Series since 1967 by beating the Brewers, who were then in the American League. Willie McGee, a rookie then, had a fabulous Game Three, hitting two home runs and saving a home run and another extra-base hit in center field. But the

Cardinals caught a playoff break at the start of their quest. Atlanta Braves knuckleballer Phil Niekro had the Cardinals shut out 1–0 into the fifth inning of Game One of the best-of-five National League Championship Series, but then it rained. The rules are different now, and the game would have continued. But this one was postponed—not resumed—and the Braves were shut out 7–0 by Bob Forsch in the next game, which went into the books as the official Game One.

The Cardinals won Game Two in the bottom of the ninth inning—Niekro came back to pitch in this one—on a hit by Ken Oberkfell and then scored four runs in the second inning at Atlanta to win Game Three before the Braves' fans even had a chance to get involved.

It's been 60 years since I broke into the majors. Probably the biggest change in that time was the AstroTurf, going to it in the first place and then doing away with it. That made for a much faster game. And Ozzie Smith changed the game, too. He was the first defensive player I remember who was always on the move when he caught the ball. We were taught a three-point stance in our defense. But he was on the move before the pitch.

Everybody is worried about sign stealing these days. Well, call for a curveball, and when the hitter's leaning in for it, throw a fastball. Knock him down. That will change that stuff right away. But nobody knocks anybody down. I told one of our catchers, Mike Matheny, one time about doing this. He said, "Oh, I couldn't do that."

I said, "Why not?"

I just learned the game differently; that's all. They say you can't throw at a guy anymore. The hell you can't. The players are more athletic today. There's no doubt about that. But they're not better—because they don't have to be better. In the olden days, you had to be better because you had to be tough. The guy who was tough persevered. Perseverance and character were two words you used. Now you've got pitchers up here who shouldn't be up here in my mind. We've had guys come from A ball to Triple A to the big leagues. Look at what we had on the Cardinals last year: 29 walks with the bases loaded. That's the stuff you learn in the minor leagues. You don't walk a guy with the bases loaded. You make him put the ball in play. That aggravates me. But the game has changed, so you just accept it. You have three-pitch innings sometimes. That should never happen if you're on offense. And when the shift is put on, why not bunt for a hit when you're two runs down? A guy's going to hit a two-run homer with nobody on base?

One thing that hasn't changed is me wearing black, though I can't tell you when it started. More than anything, it's the jacket. I wear a black jacket all the time no matter how hot it is. And if it wears out, I get another black jacket. Have you ever seen a man in a desert without a coat? Everybody wears a coat in the desert. Think about it. You never see a guy in the desert without a coat. The protection against the sun is just as important as it is against the cold. It's where I carry my stuff, too, like my glasses and my phone. I carry my phone on the inside left, and my glasses are on my inside right and I put my sunglasses in another pocket.

DAL MAXVILL

I was Mike Shannon's teammate on the St. Louis Cardinals from 1963 to 1970 and the team's general manager from 1985 to 1995. I had great confidence in Mike as a player and as a teammate. And when he was broadcasting and I was general manager, I trusted him when we had conversations about players. I knew he was going to be a straight shooter the whole way and I knew he wasn't going to try to blow up anything or try to make something out of nothing.

After he moved to third base in 1967–70, we played side by side for three years with me at shortstop. I understand he told a story of me saying he should bounce his throws to Orlando Cepeda at first base because Cepeda had trouble seeing the high throw. I might have made some sort of wise-acre remark about it, but I don't even know why Mike would say that I said, "Bounce it over to him." I wish I could back up that story, but as we all know, "Moon Man" dances to his own tune and always did his whole life.

That nickname goes all the way back to the minor leagues—at least that's the way I heard it. Whenever Sputnik was going on back in the late 1960s, a couple of his teammates were talking about how strange it was that something was up there circling the planet. One of them said, "You know Shannon's up there, too. He's around the moon all the time." That's how I believe the nickname came about, but I can't back it up. I also heard that he was talking to Bob Gibson during a game about "Someday, there's going to be a man on the moon." So there are some different origin stories for his nickname. But whatever the source, it's a very apropos title. "Moon Man" fits him perfectly.

One example was when Mickey Mantle hit the game-winning homer off Barney Schultz in the World Series, and Mike leaped against the low box-seats in right field, trying to make the catch, even though the ball was in the upper deck. "Moon" was going to give it everything he had. Crazy man. He's a wonderfully crazy man, that's for damn sure. We've all heard his radio Moonisms or Shannonisms, like when he said, "And the standing-room only crowd settles back into their seats." You can't make up stuff like that. It's beautiful.

He was strong as an ox and could go all night, and as telecaster Jay Randolph put it: he was "America's Guest." He could come in at 1:00 or 2:00 AM after broadcasting a game and then get everybody up at 5:00 or 6:00 to go golfing. Then he'd finish golfing, go have a meal, and then come to the ballpark, do a game that night, and then do the same thing again the next morning.

Over 50 years he's made a big impact on Cardinals baseball. Bottom line: he's loved. Whenever I go anywhere and the conversation goes to Cardinals baseball, the name Shannon comes up. It is amazing the popularity level that he has attained and maintained for 50 years. He was very popular as a player and then had the health situation with nephritis, which was a very scary thing for him. And then nobody—and I mean nobody on this planet—thought he could go into the booth and do the job that he did and do it for 50 years.

I mean, come on. No. 1, it's not that easy. And for him to be able to do that was just wonderful. When he first came up with nephritis and he was under Stan London's care, trying to recover, his first wife, Judy, called and asked me if I would mind taking Mike goose hunting out at Black Swan Lake by Kansas City. We had gone out there several years prior to that. She said that Mike was struggling a little bit but was optimistic about recovery. I set it up with my good buddy out in Lexington, Missouri. I went over and picked Mike up at his house on a Friday morning and I was a bit surprised by his appearance. He was quite a bit heavier. His color was not good. He had that yellowish look to him.

In the three days we were there, Mike said every time we were getting ready to go out to hunt that he was tired. So we stayed around the motel, and every time we checked on him, he was in bed. He kept saying we should go hunting without him, but we never did. We made the four-hour drive back to St. Louis on Sunday—he slept all the way back—and when I dropped him off, he said, "We'll do it again sometime, Dal." Judy asked how it went, and I said that Mike had slept pretty much the whole time, and we never did get a chance to go hunting.

She teared up and thanked us for giving it a shot. I came back home and told my wife that Mike wasn't in real good shape. Well, Moon Man came back. Later on, when he was announcing and feeling much better, he looked me and with that cackle he had, and said, "Maxie, don't worry about me, babe. I'm like a cat with nine lives and I've only used up one of them."

Is that beautiful or what?

From then on, Moon was his happy, crazy self with everybody. You'd go into a hotel, and the next thing you knew, he's got them setting up a bar over in the corner, and we're going to have a party. I was in several of those drinking sessions, especially after day games in San Francisco or Chicago. There were times when, as I recall, we did not make curfew. If there was a curfew at midnight, we missed that by several digits many times.

Our manager, Red Schoendienst, understood that. We were in the World Series for several years there. When you do stuff like that and you're winning, you're called colorful. If you do that kind of stuff when you're finishing in fifth place all the time, you're troublemakers. You go from colorful to troublemakers rather quickly depending on the performance of the team.

But you could still have fun at lunch. Mike called me one morning in San Francisco and said Roger Maris had just called Joe DiMaggio and that we're going down to have lunch at Joe's restaurant at Fisherman's Wharf. I said, "Are you serious?"

And he said, "Maris is good friends of DiMaggio."

For me, DiMaggio is kind of a Stan Musial, so I said, "I've got to see this."

Mike and I both just sat there and listened to Maris and DiMaggio relay stories about their times with the New York Yankees. It was one of my favorite luncheons of all time. It was the first time I'd ever seen Mike sit and listen most of the way. Usually, he was waving his baton and leading the parade. But Mike made that possible for me. That was Mike. Big heart. Fun to be with. But when he was playing, he was dead serious from the time they played the National Anthem until the game was over. He was a real gamer back then.

One time we were in St. Louis and we're out there on the field, and they're playing the National Anthem. We're kind of standing close to each other, and when the anthem was over, he looked at me and said, "What inning is it?"

I'm thinking, *They just played the National Anthem. What inning do you think it is? It's the first inning.*

After I looked at him for a second, he had that sly grin on his face like, *I know what inning it is, babe.*

He made things more enjoyable wherever he went, that's for sure.

CHAPTER 8

My All-Time Teams

I consider Babe Ruth the best player ever in the game—certainly the best player I didn't see play. He was hitting 60 home runs when no other team in the league was hitting 60 home runs. That happened in 1927. Statistically, he just knocks everybody down. Plus, he was the best pitcher in the game for three or four years. He was just bigger and stronger than most guys. He could outdo everybody in everything. I would have liked to have seen him play and have him on *Live at Shannon's* after the game. No telling where that would have gone.

Nobody wanted to tick him off when he played. If he got mad, then he might have hit three home runs in a game instead of two. I know you can't compare eras. But I can't believe anybody was better than Ruth. Stan Musial could go into the outfield with Ruth and Willie Mays. Now, that's a pretty good outfield, but I'm going to put Musial on my all-time team at first base because he played more than 1,000 games both at first base and in the outfield. And I want to get Henry Aaron in the outfield. Ruth, Mays, Aaron. Pretty easy. That's a no-brainer there. I don't think you can argue with that.

Mays is the best player I've ever seen because he could do everything. He was also probably the smartest player I ever played against. I mentioned how smart I thought he was to Tom Seaver of the New York Mets one time, and he said I was right. Mays was basically finished with the Mets by that point. His talent was completely diminished at the time in 1973 when the Mets won the pennant, but he still did some good things, and it was extraordinary how smart he was. He could dominate a game. Like when Vinegar Bend Mizell was pitching for us—he wasn't good at holding runners on—Mays would walk, steal second, steal third, and steal home. He knew he had to steal second on the first pitch, third on the second pitch, and home on the third pitch.

Here is a word you never hear in this game: balance. Well, he had balance, which was very important for a hitter. If they threw at me, I got away and went down. Other guys might have just moved their heads because they had better balance, and Mays was one of those because he was afraid of the ball. But he had so much talent. And he hit the ball hard. That Astroturf in St. Louis was wet one day when I was playing third base, and I just got my head turned when a ball he hit went off my cheek. It could have been much worse. I don't know what they scored that—hit or error. I wasn't thinking about that. But I had outsmarted myself on where I figured the ball would go to.

Where you really saw his balance was as a defensive player. You know what I never saw Mays do? Leave his feet in the outfield. I saw him leave his feet when he'd go to the wall. But I never saw him leave his feet when he could dive for a ball. He would catch it off the grass, but he would never leave his feet. But at the wall—they had a cyclone fence at Candlestick Park in San Francisco—he would jump and stick his foot about five feet up on that fence and make the catch. That looked dangerous, but he never got hurt doing it.

We remained friends long after we were through playing. He would always ask me to come down and see him when we were broadcasting in San Francisco. For some reason, we always got along great. He was getting almost blind later in life. And when I would go down there, it wouldn't be long before he would look up the clock and say, "We've got to go." But I knew he couldn't see that clock. So I would pick up a drink he had and move it and he couldn't find it for a while. Not everybody you could do that with, but I enjoyed sparring and kidding with Mays.

Speaking of balance as a hitter, Big Mac, Mark McGwire, taught me a lot about that. He was a really good hitting coach with the St. Louis Cardinals and then the Los Angeles

Dodgers. Not that many hitters had the balance that he had. But he really didn't have enough hits to make my all-time team, and I have to leave Tony Perez off, too, at first base. But when he played with the Cincinnati Reds, Perez absolutely was the one guy I didn't want to see up there when I was playing third base. He would hit the ball that was behind him, and I could never see it coming off the bat. He was the best RBI guy I ever saw—especially with a guy at first and two outs when he would hit one of those gappers to right-center or left-center.

I might surprise you with this one, but I've got Pete Rose at second base on my team. He really could play anywhere, but this is where he broke in during the early 1960s. He might not get in the Hall of Fame but he's still my second baseman. After all, he had more than 4,200 hits. He could do anything he wanted to do. He could hit a home run if he had to. I remember his old roommate, somebody who was on our team, knocked him down with a pitch, and Rose got up and hit a home run over the left-field wall.

"Let's play two." That's what Ernie Banks of the Chicago Cubs always would say whenever we came to Wrigley Field in Chicago. It seemed like all of Banks' 512 homers just got over the wall and landed in the front row of the bleachers, but he hit them, didn't he? I know Banks played a lot of first base later on, but I recall him best as a shortstop. Five hundred home runs? That was relatively easy to pick Banks.

No question that Mike Schmidt of the Philadelphia Phillies was the best at third base—both defensively and offensively. I bet you didn't know Schmidt hit .196 in his first full season in the majors in 1973. Then he won the league home run title the next three seasons, and the rest was history as he finished with 548 homers.

As the closer, even though Lee Smith was awfully good, you have to go with Mariano Rivera of the New York Yankees. In the Hall of Fame voting over the years, I think some voters just don't vote for a guy to prevent a unanimous selection, but in Rivera's case, he got every vote. You can't argue with that.

Bob Gibson is on my all-time team and, of course, the Cardinals team, too, as the right-handed pitcher. Hall of Fame. Seven World Series wins. More than 3,000 strikeouts. Had the 1.12 ERA in 1968. Need I say more?

Sandy Koufax of the Dodgers is my left-handed pitcher and he had to be good to beat out my old teammate, Steve Carlton, who achieved most of his success with the Phillies after we traded him away. That's a pretty freakin' good team. How about Koufax? He wins 25, 26, and 27 in three of his final four seasons. He wins five straight ERA titles and strikes out 300 or more in three of his last four seasons. And then he quits at age 31 because his elbow was killing him.

Johnny Bench is the catcher. Maybe he wasn't as good as some at putting down the fingers, but he had a great arm and great power. He had almost 400 homers and 1,400 RBIs and had 40 or more homers twice. And the Big Red Machine of the mid-1970s started with him at the switch.

Tony La Russa is the manager. He would understand the players a little more than some of the others. And he made some moves sometimes that didn't seem to make a lot of sense, but he didn't want to lose a World Series. So he would sacrifice one game for the bigger picture.

But just think of some of the managers we've had with the Cardinals—La Russa, Whitey Herzog, Red Schoendienst. They're all Hall of Famers. And when Joe Torre went to the Yankees, he won four World Series and he went into the Hall of Fame, too. Torre was made for managing in New York. He was so much better in New York. But he had the players, too. As a manager he was really good at what managers are supposed to be good at. He put the players in the right place. That's the idea of a manager.

But what separated La Russa is that he planned on a World Series every year. He went to spring training planning that. And he was deadly serious. When he and Dusty Baker got into it in Chicago when Dusty was managing the Cubs,

I didn't take any side. La Russa said, "I thought you were my friend. I thought you were a Cardinal."

I told him, "He's my friend and so are you. I keep my friends." La Russa holds grudges, let's put it that way.

I disagreed with La Russa on a lot of stuff, but I picked him as my all-time manager and on my all-time Cardinals team, too. He was in three World Series here and three more with the Oakland A's. And he is 3–3 overall. On the other hand, Red Schoendienst was one of the few to play on a World Series winner (1946), manage one (1967), and coach on two (1964 and 1982).

That 1982 game had a strange finish in that Bruce Sutter, who had a three-run lead in the ninth inning against the Milwaukee Brewers in Game Seven, shook off the signature pitch that got him to the Hall of Fame. Sutter was the greatest split-fingered pitch pitcher of all time, maybe, but he shook off Darrell Porter to throw his 85 mile-per-hour fastball. Gorman Thomas, the hitter, couldn't believe it. He struck out to end the game and the series, and Herzog had his only World Series title, even though I—and he—think his 1985 and maybe 1987 teams were better but didn't win. All that shaking off, why didn't Thomas figure it out? Oh well.

On my all-time Cardinals team, I would have Musial in the outfield. I'd put him in left. There's some tough decisions there. But I'm going to list three outfielders, no matter their position. I've got Musial and Lou Brock; that's automatic. Boy, Brock was one tough guy. Koufax broke Brock's collarbone with a pitch after Brock had tried to bunt on him. Brock was out only like two days. Then, of course, you've got the 3,000 hits and the 938 stolen bases, and he was the catalyst of those three championship teams we had in 1964, 1967, and 1968 And now, we come to Joe Medwick, who I never got to see play. But he must have been pretty good to win the Triple Crown in 1937. That was the last time that anybody won the Triple Crown in the National League. You know Medwick had had an unbelievable 95 extra-base hits in 1936 and did even better than that with 97 in 1937. That was the year he led in everything. He had 10 triples, too. But the big numbers were .374 average with 31 homers and 154 RBIs.

Still, I went with Jim Edmonds as my other outfielder to go with Brock and Musial. I remember my son, Tim, calling and telling me after the Cardinals' trade with the Anaheim Angels was made. He said, "You've got a guy coming here who plays too shallow in the outfield, and the other players didn't like that."

That guy went back on a ball as well as everybody I've ever seen. But maybe his best catch was when he went to the side and back into left-center to make a diving catch against the Houston Astros in Game Seven of the National League Championship Series in 2004 to keep the game close. Edmonds had won the sixth game with a homer in the 12th inning, but the Cardinals were down 1–0 in the second inning of Game Seven, and it could have been worse as the Houston Astros put two runners on base.

Guys like my teammate, Curt Flood, and Willie McGee, were great center fielders who started with their backs against the paint on the outfield wall. Edmonds liked to start right behind second base. But if he doesn't make that catch on Brad Ausmus, the game is over, and the Cardinals don't go to the World Series. It's that simple. He had a great jump and he basically ran the ball down to where he could dive and make the play. He was a good hitter, too. In my mind, he could take the whole season off and come back with no practice at all and still be successful because he had really good hands. No, he had great hands. The tip-off on Edmonds is in his OPS. For five straight seasons from 2000 to 2004, he had at least a .974 OPS and twice in that time was over 1.000.

I almost took Nolan Arenado at third base over Kenny Boyer and Scott Rolen. I know Arenado's only been here a year, but he makes every play, drives in 100 runs, and hits 35 homers. He doesn't really have a weakness in the field, and his arm is unbelievably strong and quick. But those other two guys were really good, too. And I played with Boyer, so I'm going to use that as a tiebreaker.

The best defensive player we had on last year's team wasn't even Arenado, and he's won a Gold Glove every year he's played. It was the first baseman, Paul Goldschmidt, who makes the entire defense better the way he handles throws over there at the bag and he started some incredible double plays. He saved more errors than anybody else I saw. Without a doubt, he was the best defensive player we had because he had more chances. The more chances you have, the more chances you have to screw up. But this all-Cardinals team is tough to pick, and he won't be able to crack it either. The clue is that it's a six-letter word, starting with P.

At shortstop on the all-Cardinals team, I've got to take Ozzie Smith. But believe it or not, Smith was a better hitter than he was a fielder. He turned out to be a better offensive player than a defensive player because he had lost some of his range when he had his rotator cuff arm problem and couldn't throw from the hole like he used to. Nobody really ever thought about his offense versus his defense, but they should have. And as far as I'm concerned, he's the best PR person that baseball has ever had. Smith knew what he was doing. When the Cardinals got Terry Pendleton to play third base with good range to his left, he could shade up the middle, taking away some hits there and also not having to strain his arm as much throwing from the hole.

Smith suffered his torn rotator cuff in 1985 but chose not to have the full-blown surgery that Boston Red Sox shortstop Rick Burleson had. Burleson, who was a great player, never was the same again after having his surgery a couple of years earlier, and Smith had taken note of that. Smith's shoulder had been deteriorating gradually for a few years, and he had difficulty making the long throw for several seasons. So he got by with a quicker release and playing to his left. But by the time he finally had arthroscopic surgery in 1995, Smith had reached the point where he had gotten 10 more years out of his arm and was well on his way to the Hall of Fame.

The Cardinals have had a bunch of great shortstops, including Musial's and Schoendienst's old teammate, Marty Marion, who was the MVP of the National League in 1944. And then there was Garry Templeton, who might have had more raw talent than any of them but reportedly had problems with some chemicals and he also had some problems with Herzog, too. Herzog, who famously pulled him down the dugout steps on a hot day in St. Louis after Templeton had flipped off some fans, finally had had enough and traded him to the San Diego Padres for Smith after the 1981 season. It all started when Templeton, who was playing with a sore leg, didn't run out a third strike, which had eluded the catcher. Herzog had told Templeton before the game not to strain himself, but it looked bad when the ball was all the way back at the screen, and Templeton wasn't running. If Templeton had La Russa as his manager, how much better would he have been? How much patience would La Russa even have had?

Schoendienst was one of my longtime friends and one of the greatest Cardinals ever, but I've got to go with Rogers Hornsby at second base. I didn't see him, of course, but how can you not choose Hornsby? He won seven batting titles, hit .370 or better six times as a Cardinal and .400 or better three times, and had more than 2,900 hits. Schoendienst gets honorable mention.

Since we've got Musial in the outfield, we've got an opening at first, and I'm going to put Albert Pujols there. I thought he would be a better defender than some of the others but not as good as Keith Hernandez, who was the best defender we've had at first base during my time in St. Louis and is honorable mention on my all-Cardinals team. He was a little different defender than—let's say—Orlando Cepeda. I had no idea that Cepeda, who was a great hitter and leader for our teams in the '60s, had trouble with infield throws that were eye high or higher. One day I threw one that went between his ear and his glove. I said to shortstop Dal Maxvill, "What's going on here?"

He said, "Bounce it."

They say that first base is easy. It's hard. But Pujols was a natural there. Besides, he drove in over 100 runs for 10 seasons in a row and missed by one RBI in 2011, which was his final year with the Cardinals. That was also the only year of the 11 he didn't hit .300, and that was a near miss at .299. He hit .359 at his best and he wasn't getting many infield hits when he was doing that because he didn't run that well, though he was a very smart base runner and excellent base stealer. I don't see how you can have anybody over Pujols at first base. And don't forget those three homers he hit in one game in Game Three of the 2011 World Series in Texas.

Yadier Molina is my catcher. We've had some great ones here. It depends on what you want. Offense? Choose Ted Simmons. Defense? Choose Molina, who became a good hitter later in his career. He had five .300 seasons. You could go with a combination of good hitter/good receiver in my old teammate, Tim McCarver, but I'm taking Molina with Simmons as my honorable mention. I judge catchers by how they call a game. If they hit, it's a bonus as far as I'm concerned. You can help win a game more by putting down fingers than you can by hitting. Pitchers are like doctors and lawyers. Every guy specializes in something.

Gibson, of course, is my all-time Cardinals right-hander, too, besides being on my major league all-time team. But Adam Wainwright and Bob Forsch would have been closer to No. 1 on some other team. You've got to take Forschie as an honorable mention choice because he was the only pitcher in the history of the Cardinals to have two no-hitters. Forschie was a tough SOB. He hit Jeffrey Leonard of the San Francisco Giants in a league championship game after Leonard had been hitting home runs here, running around the bases with his arm in the infamous one flap down position. Forsch hit him right in the butt, and the Cardinals came back to win that third game out at Candlestick Park, and that proved to be a pivotal game in the series.

In my day, they used to hit you in the back if you did something like Leonard did. I must have played in the toughest times. Those guys would even throw at your head and wouldn't give a damn. That's the way I was taught. And when they hit you, it wasn't like it got away from them. They knew exactly what they were doing. I remember the first time I batted against Don Drysdale of the Dodgers. He threw me two perfect pitches on the outside of the plate, so I shortened up in my swing, and I hit a little line drive single to right field. The next time up, he knocked me on my can. He was right. I was cheatin'. And I accepted it. Nowadays, you wouldn't accept it.

Wainwright still is pitching, so who knows where he will wind up? He's already had two seasons of 20 wins and two more of 19, which is hard to do these days. To me, he was the Cardinals' Most Valuable Player in 2021 at age 40. He stopped so many losing streaks it was unbelievable. That's really what a Most Valuable Player is. If it wasn't for him, we'd have been dead and gone last year.

The best left-hander I played with was "Lefty" Carlton, but he had his bigger years with the Phillies. So my lefthander on the Cardinals' team is John Tudor, who just went into the club's Hall of Fame last year. Tudor was 21–8 in 1985 when the Cardinals won the National League East, holding off the New York Mets, and then the National League Championship Series. But how he got there was remarkable. He was 1–7 in June and then won 20 of his final 21, pitching 10 shutouts in the process. For his five seasons with the team, he was 62–26 for a percentage over .700, and very few pitchers can maintain that kind of mark.

For closers, Lee Smith is right there as my top pick, I would tell you that. But that's a tough one. You've got Sutter, who is a very strong honorable mention. Then there was Todd Worrrell, Trevor Rosenthal, Jason Motte, Dennis Eckersley, and Tom Henke, who pitched only one year with the Cardinals. There's also Al Hrabosky and even Joe Hoerner, who didn't have a lot of saves on our 1960s teams but was a terrific closer. But Big Lee averaged 44 saves a year for four years. That breaks the tie. If I was picking an expansion team, the first player I would pick would be the closer. Nothing makes a team more disgruntled than having a lead into the last inning and then blowing it.

Now, if the all-time team, which had Gibson as one of its starters, faced the all-time Cardinals team, which had Gibson as one of its starters, Gibson would have to face Koufax. And I'd still take Gibson. The Cardinals would win it—because of Gibson. To mess with Gibson, I'm actually going to say there's a four-way tie for best Cardinals manager—La Russa, Schoendienst, Herzog, and Solly Hemus. Gibson couldn't stand Hemus, who had put Gibson in the bullpen. He hated that guy for that and a few other things. (Gibson also thought Hemus was a bit racially insensitive.)

Having said all this, you really can't compare one era to another. But I think the best era in baseball was right after World War II because of the influence of Black players, and there were only eight teams in each league.

Would I have made the all-Cardinals team as a reserve? Yeah, if they needed somebody to be the No. 3 catcher. I could catch well enough in an emergency. I could save them a spot on the roster. I could play outfield, infield, and catcher. I always thought I had the best arm in right field—better than even Roberto Clemente of the Pittsburgh Pirates.

When I was a minor leaguer in camp, they put me up against Gene Green, another guy with a good arm who was with the Cardinals, and I outthrew him in both arm strength and accuracy. The manager at the time, Fred Hutchinson, was a tough guy. After watching me, he said to the general manager, "Don't let that animal out of here."

That was a great compliment, coming from Hutch.

Oh yes, my Cardinals team would need a general manager. How about Musial, who filled the job for only one year in 1967 and then retired? We won the World Series that year against Boston after winning the pennant by 10 ½ games. We made only one player move that year and we played for a month with just 24 guys when you could have 25. He said, "Why should we bring somebody up when he's not going to play anyway?"

I thought that was a great quote. That was a good combination—Schoendienst as the manager and Musial as the general manager. I would imagine those two got along pretty good. In fact, I know they did.

And we'll need a commissioner for my all-time team. Hands down, it's Bud Selig, who will go down in history as one of the great commissioners for some of the things he did like the wild-card team in the playoffs. Nobody liked it at first, but look at the interest that has generated.

When they look back at commissioners the way they look at presidents 20 years later, the guys in the media are going to say, "Holy mackerel. This guy was phenomenal."

What this guy did in his term was never done before and may never be done again. He's a combination of many, many things. But I think his greatest asset is that he's a tremendous communicator. He doesn't communicate in the public as well as some other orators, but when he was communicating behind the scenes with the baseball people, he was outstanding.

BUD SELIG

You know how much I like Mike Shannon. My affection for him grew over the years. He was here in Milwaukee a lot, especially when the Brewers went to the National League in the late 1990s, and the Cardinals would come in three times a year. I know a couple of times he and his wife came to see me in my office after I became commissioner.

I look at Mike the way I look at Bob Uecker, who has been broadcasting Brewers games into his late 80s. They both have been loyal to their franchises and have represented their franchises beautifully. They were both great announcers. Mike had a distinctive style, I must admit. When you're the commissioner, you have an opportunity to meet different people whom you really like. And I not only have a lot of affection for Mike, but also a lot of respect. He's a baseball man through and through. He's a Cardinal through and through. There's just something about him.

I know I like him a lot more than Herman Wehmeier or Bobby Del Greco, who used to play for the Cardinals in 1956. They broke my heart when Wehmeier pitched and Del Greco made a great catch to beat the Milwaukee Braves, my favorite team, in a big game in late September in 1956. A month before he died, my great friend, Henry Aaron, said, "Commissioner, we should have won four straight pennants."

And I said to him, "What about 1956?"

And he said, "Del Greco never made catches like that, and Wehmeier probably never got anybody out again."

Henry never got over it. And I never got over it. But I was pleased to learn that Mike had placed Henry on his all-time baseball team. That was wonderful. I know that Mike saw Henry play enough, so he knows how great Henry was. Henry was somewhat appreciated and should have been more so. He played in Milwaukee and Atlanta. Not totally different from Mike's great friend, Stan Musial, who played in St. Louis for all those years. There's something about guys who play in New York and Los Angeles, who just get a lot more recognition. But you talk about Aaron and Musial and then Shannon and Uecker and you can see that greatness isn't just reserved for the East Coast and West Coast.

Mike is a man of many opinions, and on plenty of occasions, he had ideas on how we could improve the game. He was gentle, of course. We had great conversations and talked about a lot of things. You know, when I thought of Mike Shannon, I thought of the Cardinals in St. Louis. He was so good, so distinctive. If I was responsible for Uecker here when I ran the Brewers, I interpret that as a great compliment. He and Mike both did what you wanted them to do. They were both great baseball guys who loved the game. But they really represented their hometown team. When you think of the Brewers, you think of Uecker, don't you? And when you think of Shannon, who better represented the culture of St. Louis, its fans, the players, everybody, than Mike Shannon? Nobody.

I think you can tell exactly how I feel about him.

There were times when I was getting banged around as commissioner for any number of things, and he was very supportive. He would say, "Don't let the [bleeps] get you down."

I have grown to love Mike. I agreed with him a lot, which some may say may not always be good. But I look at it as good. But I want to make one point: watching him, listening to him...what you saw is what you got. They can't pay a greater compliment than that.

We all grew up with radio and guys like Vin Scully or Harry Caray or Joe Garagiola. Mike is in that class. There's no question about it. And so is Uecker. But all these guys are in the Hall of Fame wing for broadcasters, and Mike isn't. He absolutely should be. Why is that? We ought to try to do something about that. If I can do anything, I will because he clearly belongs in the Hall of Fame. Clearly. Anyone would be a candidate if you were in the business for 50 years and were mediocre. But he was far from mediocre. He was great.

CHAPTER 9

My Restaurants

I've had several restaurants while I've been broadcasting. It's been a venture I got into about 25 years ago because Joe Fresta, who went to high school with me at Christian Brothers College, asked me to join him. I said yes because I wanted to diversify my portfolio. I could have just stuck to broadcasting, but I'm not one to stand still. I've never made any kind of decision where it was temporary. In other words, if I made up my mind to do something, I made it up to do it for a long time. It was a permanent situation with me.

At first, I had no money at all in the downtown venture, which was near the ballpark and which ultimately became a Hooters. Just my name was involved. I had turned down Fresta numerous times. I didn't know anything about the restaurant business when I got into it. I do now. Eventually, when the opportunity became available, I bought out my partners when we moved our location once the new ballpark was built in 2006. That timing was perfect, just in time to host a World

Series, which the Cardinals won. The ballpark moved two blocks south. And so did we. It all worked out very well.

The restaurants—whether they were downtown or in Edwardsville, Illinois, or the one at St. Louis Lambert International Airport—have all been successful. Whatever I go into, I'm into it 100 percent. I don't take no for an answer. Failure isn't in my vocabulary unless I'm batting three or four times in a game against Don Drysdale.

My wife, Lori, runs the one in Edwardsville now and she's got that one succeeding to the point where I should have let her do so a long time ago. I wanted a family member in there because I thought that was the best way to do it, but we're looking for somebody else to run it now. We're still looking at starting another restaurant, too…but nothing yet.

Some athletes or former athletes, who got into the restaurant business didn't go into it 100 percent. They lent their name to it, but that's all. But I just don't put my name to it. I put me to it. And I think that's one of the big reasons our restaurants have been successful. I looked at it differently than most athletes who went into the restaurant business. Most thought of that move as only temporary. They'd show up once in a while and shake hands and they figured that's all they had to do. I used to go over to the restaurant downtown before and after the games. The people expected to see me there, and they wanted to see all the memorabilia that we had on hand. I still have enough memorabilia for future restaurants, let's put it that way. Pictures, baseballs, etc. Most of the baseballs are in our Edwardsville location.

We've got some stuff at the airport location, and the largest amount of sales come from that location, which is in the A concourse. It's not the main concourse, like the Southwest or the C concourse. I don't know really how it happened, but that amount of money generated from there is great.

We had two prime corner locations downtown for many years—whether they were near Busch Stadium II or Busch Stadium III. Fans gathered before and after the game, and often we'd have a radio show, *Live at Shannon's*, at the restaurant on a weekend night after a game with some of the top names in baseball and even in the entertainment and business arenas as guests.

Those shows were tremendously successful both for the people who were in the restaurant at the time and the radio listeners all across the country.

Most of the guests might not have been playing anymore, but we had a lot of managers, like Dusty Baker, when he was with any of a number of teams, or Joe Maddon on the show. Maddon, who came through many times when he managed the Chicago Cubs, grew up in Pennsylvania as a great St. Louis Cardinals fan and an even greater Stan Musial fan. Musial, by the way, once told me, "I've met 10,000 people who told me they were from Donora, Pennsylvania, where I grew up, and the population of the town was only 1,100."

We had the Big Unit, Hall of Fame left-hander Randy Johnson, on the show because he was so diversified. He had other interests, and that's what I want to have in my guests. He got into photography and he wanted to talk about things other than baseball; so we did. But he came to me one day and said he needed to talk to Bob Gibson and asked if I could introduce him. Where does a guy like Johnson go when he has a pitching issue? I know if I was the Big Unit and I had a pitching question, I would have gone to Gibson, too.

On the shows I liked to have people who could drink and talk. That went along with the deal. They could drink during the show and they could eat steaks or shrimp or both afterward. A guy like Gibson was a great guest. We didn't like having people who couldn't drink and talk at the same time. One of the most interesting shows was when they had the Midnight Ramble of nude bicyclists going down Market Street outside, and I could see them out the front window. I couldn't believe it, and Mike Claiborne, who was hosting the show, couldn't believe it either. We don't have the downtown restaurant anymore, but the Midnight Ramble continues on Market Street just across from where our building was. I still don't get it, but who am I to say?

There were a couple of other good shows that we had with Hollywood people. Billy Bob Thornton was on one night. That was a good one, and he was pretty well-behaved. We never really had to "bleep" anyone out. Maybe we should have, but we didn't.

We were on at midnight and beyond, which is an unusual time for a show. Bobby Cox, the great Atlanta manager, used to listen to us on a Friday or Saturday night when he had a 30-minute drive home from his games in Atlanta. He would flip on KMOX Radio 1120 and he would laugh and laugh. We did the show from the ballpark this past season. It was easier to do it there.

You didn't really know where the show was going sometimes. But that's because when you're talking to someone, you find some things out you had no idea about. They also know I'm not going to back them into a corner. And it always helps to have a drink or two, let's be honest about it. I would say those shows, along with conversations we had with people during rain delays, were the things I enjoyed the most about my 50 years in broadcasting. People ask me which three all-time baseball guys I would want on my show, and I say Gibson would be No. 1; Bill White, who was on our World Series winner in 1964 and used to be the National League president, would be No. 2; and the late Curt Flood, our great center fielder, would be No. 3. But I don't know about Flood drinking. I know Gibson could drink and I know White could drink and talk. We always found a way to drink.

As far as guys I never met, how about Babe Ruth, the greatest player ever? And the Wright brothers. Ruth probably would be in a for a steak and a couple of beers and a little ball talk. And if the Wright brothers couldn't make it to the show, I would take them down to Houston to the space center, put them on the hill, and have them watch the spacecraft take off.

I wouldn't talk to them. I just would listen. Can you imagine the conversation? Orville Wright would be telling people, "I told you so."

A lot of the people in the restaurant wanted to sit as close to the table, where we were doing the show, as possible, so they could feel a part of it, or they wanted to sit close to where the speakers in the restaurant were or where there wasn't as much clattering of dishes. That would be a fun show to reincarnate.

Looking at the restaurant business, in general, I interviewed Joe DiMaggio, who had a restaurant in San Francisco, and asked him, "Why are you still in the business?"

He said, "I consider myself a connoisseur of fine dining. The only way you can fine dine in this game is to own your own place." Basically, he was right.

We got out of our downtown spot about five or six years ago, but we've become very happy with the people in Edwardsville. They've taken a lot of pride in it, and we got a new chef who used to be in the White House. I've had three restaurants before and I will have three restaurants again someday soon. And then I'll open up a fourth, a fifth, and a sixth down the road. The restaurant business is where I'm planning on making money. It's nice to be doing something else when you're making money. It's not easy, but it's nice. You take the good with the bad. And you just try to turn the bad into good. Sometimes it works, and sometimes it doesn't.

There's a different kind of enjoyment running a restaurant than playing in a big game or broadcasting a big game. You can have fun in the restaurant business if you look at it the right way. Making money is fun, and that's part of it. Red Schoendienst, who enjoyed the value of a dime, used to say, "I can hear that cash register all the way over here."

I had a lot to do with stuff on the menu, like having chicken livers at the restaurant in Edwardsville. I like chicken livers; that's all there is to it. Usually, a fine dining restaurant doesn't have chicken livers. But most French restaurants don't have pork. The reason I know is when the Los Angeles Dodgers came in town, Vin Scully said he couldn't find pork—he liked what they call Iowa chops here—at the French restaurant he had gone to. They're great big, thick pork chops. When he came to town, I made sure I had them. He'd already called ahead.

Restaurants are hard to make money on, and it was especially so with the COVID-19 problem that we've had.

The government was paying people to stay home for criminy sake, and restaurants really got into a bind. Restaurants were really strapped to find people to work for them, and that's still a problem. You have to be able to trust your employees, too. Everybody thinks the restaurant business is an easy business, but it's not that way. I had more anxiety entering the restaurant business than I did broadcasting or playing because I had no experience in it. I didn't have any experience in broadcasting either, but it was the same business as playing—the baseball business. But I never really thought I would "lose my shirt," as they say in the restaurant business. I don't know if that was misplaced optimism, but I was never worried about it.

In my mind people have blamed a lot of things on COVID. We let COVID run us instead of us running COVID, as far I'm concerned. And I feel a lot of people are in the same boat that I'm in, but they just can't say it. I can say it—because I just tell the truth. I've always been me. Period. Take it or leave it. You get what you get with me. I don't sugarcoat anything. That's the way I broadcast. I just tell the truth.

But I don't ever criticize the manager because I've never been a manager. I have enough respect for the game that if you haven't pushed the buttons, it doesn't count. I've been a player, so I can tell you a player misses a ball or something like that because I've made a lot of mistakes myself. Maybe a player's attention was taken away from him in one way or another. He could have been sick, injured, or didn't hit a guy particularly well. There are hundreds of reasons why he could have made that mistake, but I know from experience what I did wrong. So I can voice my opinion on that. And it's not easy, you know?

I had six kids while I was playing and broadcasting. There was once a lady who told me, "I'll tell you how old I am, but I won't tell you how old my kids are."

I thought that was kind of funny. And then I thought about it some more, and when my son, Mike, turned 60, I said, "Damn." Now I've got two sons who are over 60. And Erin is the youngest. She's in her 40s, and that's as far as I'll take it.

Most all of them got involved in sports. Tim was an excellent defensive back at USC at the same time Lou Brock Jr. was there. Later, Tim became a player agent and now he's working for a bank in acquisitions. He had his knees operated on nine times. And then he and Mike got their knees replaced at almost the same time. Anthony Munoz, the great offensive tackle at USC and a Hall of Famer in the NFL, thought Tim could have been a pro player, and I don't doubt that.

Tim actually played one year in rookie ball in the Cardinals' system at Johnson City as a third baseman. I didn't get to see him play because I was broadcasting the Cardinals' games, but he didn't hit much and got released. One day in the spring, I was watching Tim, and he got hit by a pitch and never moved.

He found out he had astigmatism. He never saw the pitch. So I knew something was wrong. I remember when he hurt his knee for the second time. He had eight operations on the one knee. He was a bad patient. Like me, I guess.

Mike was a hell of a quarterback at Indiana State, but he hurt his knee. I was at the game in the spring when he got hurt as a freshman. It was right in front of us, and his mother was with me, too. He was going to be a good player. He was big, strong, tall, and a good passer. The play he got hurt on was a broken play, and I knew he had messed up his knee ligament. That ruined his career. He never played any more after that, even though I had taken him to see a doctor who was doing those ligament transplants in Oregon. But he couldn't really help Mike play again, and Mike has been working for Anheuser-Busch almost ever since he finished college.

My third son, Dan, wasn't as big as the other two, but he played first base for a little bit in the Cardinals' system. He had a really good hitting stroke, but he wouldn't make the final commitment. Let's just say that Danny realized that the percentages for being a professional were against him. But Danny was smart enough to know where all the bodies were buried.

He also went to the brewery and he went up the ladder fast. He was the Busch brand manager.

I also had a grandson, Gary Van Matre, who was a left-handed relief pitcher in the system. He got released after one year, too, after only seven games. I didn't say anything, but how can you release a guy after one year? I saw them all in spring training but never during the season.

Peg was an amateur boxer when she was a firefighter. They called her, "Peg the Cannon Shannon," when they had the annual Fireman vs. Policeman fights for charity the night before Thanksgiving at the home of the Blues, which now is called Enterprise Center, in St. Louis. That was always a sellout crowd and a great fund-raiser for the Backstoppers, which helps families of firefighters and policemen who died doing their jobs. I watched her fight four times on that card, and she won every time. She had no previous experience. I have no idea if she had a cannon for a punch. All I know is that she won every time she fought. She was competitive.

My daughter Pat ran the downtown restaurant for me for many years, and that was no easy job. I needed somebody to keep an eye on it while I was gone broadcasting. She was a good businessperson. She wasn't as good an athlete as the others growing up. Maybe that was why she was so good business-wise. But some downtown restaurants wound up closing with the advent of Ballpark Village, the new development across from the newest of Busch Stadiums, which has several places to eat, a hotel, and some shops. That's not the reason I closed ours, though. I closed it because I'd rather be a big part of something in a small situation than a small part of a big situation.

There wasn't a lot of pressure running it, but that was the site where we probably had the best show KMOX had. It was the one Claiborne and I put on late at night. It was kind of a landmark show—I guess it was my idea—but nobody else really had it. I had no idea whatsoever it would be as successful as it became. It just happened. It was a good break for Claiborne because it basically showed his ability—he had a lot of abilities—and that led to other strengths that he had. He just went into the Missouri Sports Hall of Fame last November.

Claiborne, by the way, had the nicest things to say about me. "No one is like him. No one will ever be like him. When I worked with Mike, I never knew in which direction it would head. He had a sixth sense about the game, being a former player and athlete. He sees things that most of us never even thought about. He sees the game from a different angle than most commoners would ever imagine. He's got this homespun approach that makes everybody who's listening to a game feel like they're sitting right next to him on the back porch or on the couch. They haven't missed anything because he makes them feel like he's talking to you directly and not everybody else. And nothing stopped him. He stared death in the eye on multiple occasions. He's the only guy who gets more than nine lives. Even cats genuflect to him."

Our final child was Erin, who wasn't necessarily an athlete, but she married a pro football coach. Gregg Williams has been a head coach with the Buffalo Bills and a top defensive coach with the Houston Oilers, Tennessee Titans, Washington Redskins, Jacksonville Jaguars, New Orleans Saints, New York Jets, St. Louis Rams, and Cleveland Browns. And he might turn up with somebody else this season.

I've been fortunate twice with my marriages. My first wife, Judy, who died of brain cancer, was wonderful. But when you've got six children and you had to tell them that their mother has a brain tumor…that's not easy at all. She fought as hard as she could, but she died one year and one day later after she found out. It was the wrong kind of brain cancer, where you couldn't operate.

She was an amazing person and so is Lori, my second wife. She's a travel agent and she's taken me places I thought I never would go to, like West Africa, where I rode an elephant. I've ridden an elephant, a horse, and a camel. I've been to six continents with her. She asked me one day, "Do you like to travel?"

I said, "Hell, no, I don't like to travel."

But traveling to play baseball in Cincinnati or Atlanta or Philadelphia or Milwaukee or Houston or Pittsburgh is different than traveling to see something. And I liked it.

She'd say, "Do you want to go to this place or that place?" And I'd say, "No."

But I ended up really enjoying it.

Some guys get lucky in other marriages and other guys don't is the only way I can explain this. Can you imagine me on an elephant? Or how do you think the elephant felt? Now I've been about everywhere but the South Pole.

People always ask me what I would have done if I hadn't been a player and then a broadcaster and restaurant owner. I tell them I probably would have been a criminologist. My dad was an attorney and then a city prosecutor for better than 20 years. I could have been a pro football player, too, but I was a couple of years too early. Instead, I could get the big money to sign with the Cardinals. After I signed with the Cardinals, they started the American Football League to go with the NFL.

I'm a big believer in fate. And I'm a big believer in quotes. Satchel Paige, the great Hall of Fame pitcher, said, "Don't look back—because someone might be gaining on you."

So I'll proceed with my restaurant career and help the club in any capacity they want. I'll keep watching baseball, even though I won't be broadcasting because it still interests me. What interests me about baseball is the same thing that interests me about football. There's a psychological part that's big in both sports. Why do people do things and when do they do them?

VIN SCULLY

Mike's exuberance was wonderful. He would come into my booth and he would sit and he was so full of life. His every response was always so positive. Even his criticisms of things that had gone wrong—he was still positive. He was kind of raw. He would answer you immediately if you had a question.

His emotions—everything was straight from the heart. You really had a tendency to believe him. When he came into the booth, I might say something kiddingly about the St. Louis Cardinals or Whitey Herzog, and he would immediately jump on it with some kind of reply that I loved. He'd give an opinion about anybody and he was always right on the money. I not only felt a great warmth for him, but I also respected what he had to say.

My wife appreciated it very much when Mike said she could sit in his broadcast booth in St. Louis when she was having trouble with some of the fans in the stands. That was the biggest booth in the big leagues, for sure. And I certainly savored those pork chops, too.

I enjoyed him immensely and he's going to be missed. He was the leader of the brass band really and he was a fun guy to be with. He bubbles with energy and he was quick to tell you a story. He always had some scrap of information I would share on the broadcast. Because he had told me, you could believe it.

I was not with him at 12:00 or 1:00 in the morning, which were good times for him, but I would certainly see him at 5:00, 6:00, or 7:00.

He had 50 years in that booth—and people will miss him without a doubt. When you're in one position as he was for so many years, I have the feeling that a listener would turn on the radio, hear Mike's voice, and it was natural. Everything was well, and we were on our normal course. The first year without him will be a jolt. I grew up in radio. I would crawl under a four-legged radio and listen to games, and after a while, the announcers became pretty important to me. Suddenly, I tuned into a game and I didn't hear Ted Husing or I didn't hear Bill Stern, who were off doing football. And I felt the absence. I felt the difference.

I grew up listening to Mel Allen and Red Barber before I got involved in Brooklyn. It seems like when you hear the same, familiar voice every day, the world is in its proper place.

When you turn the radio on and you don't hear the voice of someone who's been talking for so long, I know from personal experience that announcer is missed. It's not just quite right. It won't be right for Cardinals fans to tune in and not hear Mike. There's just no way. I know from my experience. I had several people—there were three, haha—say it just didn't have the same feeling. And, of course, that's just habit. Once you're gone, you're gone. But they will definitely miss him.

CHAPTER 10

The Final Inning

The 2020 season was a different experience than I'd ever felt. Because of COVID-19 and the players and owners haggling, we didn't play ball until late July. For the most part, I was sequestered, but we had takeout at my restaurant in Edwardsville, Illinois, and we fed breakfast to the school children in the Edwardsville district. And it was just not the kids who couldn't afford it. It was everybody. In my generation you got up in the morning, and our parents were there and they'd cooked a nice breakfast. These kids...the father's gone, the mother's gone, they go to work early.

As far as a stoppage in play or a delay in the season, I'd been through this all before. I had stop playing because I had a kidney disease. I've been through the strikes. It was different in 2020 when nobody was in the stands. I was lucky I didn't have to come down to the ballpark to do the road games when the broadcasters had to do them at Busch Stadium off television monitors.

You've got to have fun in this game. And I don't know if it was that much fun when the players had to stay six feet apart and they had to wear a mask in the dugout. They couldn't spit like they were used to, though I'm not sure how well that was enforced. But it worked its way out. It always does; trust me. People were starved for baseball. The owners were starved. The players were starved. But most of all, the fans were starved for it. I stopped by to pick up some carry-out food one day, and a woman came out and said, "I just want to hear you talk."

The crowds had to be reduced at the start of last season, which wound up hurting the St. Louis Cardinals, who drew two million instead of three. On the other hand, it wasn't any problem in Miami if they could only let 20,000 people in. They'd love to have 20,000. That would be a sellout for them. The players, who played before no crowds in 2020, had to get used to smaller crowds, at least at first, in 2021. Like at any other time, the ones who adapted were the ones who were going to succeed. Some guys were going to fall out. The psychological part of the game was going to be bigger than ever. That's the part I like anyway.

After 50 years of this, the broadcasting game is a little different now. For instance, there are a lot of harder names to pronounce. And I had to try to get some of that enthusiasm back last year because COVID had robbed me of that. But I don't think like an 82-year-old person.

The Missouri Sports Hall at Springfield, Missouri, had a special ceremony for me last year, and that was one of the fun things. They had put a statue of me up before. I don't remember what it looked like, but it was an honor just to be considered in that "legend" category.

The Cardinals had me wave to the fans during a particular inning I worked in each of the 50 games I broadcast in 2021 at home. It got a little old, but when I thought about it a little, I had to look at it from the fans' standpoint. You've got to figure there are different fans there every night, and it was a real tribute that they did that and it was nice that Budweiser picked up on it when they sponsored me.

The club gave me a golf cart, and I wanted to thank the fans and the team, but when I got to the microphone on the field on that last Sunday of the season, I broke down as I started talking about the fans and I had to step away. The rain at Busch Stadium almost wouldn't let me retire. There was a 17-minute delay in the fourth inning and then another one later. During the first one, I got to tell some stories on the air, and that was fun. But by the second one, I was ready to go.

"I can't think of anything better than to call this game and have a party," I said to the listening audience. And indeed

I had one scheduled across the street at the Cardinal Nation restaurant in Ballpark Village.

As it turned out, so did umpiring crew chief Gerry Davis, who was retiring after 40 years in the majors and had his own party a few blocks from mine at a hotel. Though the sun was shining, Davis, who inspected the home-plate area which had taken on some rain damage, waved the game off and at 5:20 PM, two careers had ended. "It's over. Let's go have a party. It's fitting," I said. "I may not be happy in two weeks, but I'm happy now."

It had been tough before the game when they had the ceremonies for me. There were the standing ovations from the sellout Busch Stadium crowd of 46,525. Added on there was cheering and applause from both dugouts. Cardinals coach and fellow Cardinals Hall of Famer Willie McGee reached out his hand to touch mine, and Matt Carpenter, whose final game as a Cardinal was that day, too, doffed his cap, as my new golf cart, which was driven by my wife, Lori, went by on a tour around the warning track. On my first trip around the track in a different golf cart, I frankly had been overwhelmed by the courtesy shown me by the Chicago Cubs because many of their young players probably didn't know me. They were all in the dugout applauding.

When it came time to speak, I teared up and couldn't speak. I walked away from the podium and sat down. Lori assisted me. It was too emotional. I wanted to thank the fans and the players, and it was a real tribute that they were out there. I'm not like that really. My voice cracked. I was too emotional.

Bill DeWitt Jr., the chairman of the club, had been taken aback a couple of days before by something I had said. I had said off-handedly that "word on the street" was that the DeWitts were looking to sell the Cardinals, which DeWitt and his son, Bill III, the team president, flatly denied. It was just a rumor. And DeWitt Jr. answered it. And he didn't say a word about it on the field that day.

The Cardinals have been great to me. But I was hit by COVID in October 2020 and I've had much of my vibrancy stripped, though I still am going stronger than most my age who have had it. I'm what they call a long hauler. Nobody's ever come back from this crap like me. I'm going to be the first one. Everybody's telling me I'm getting better, but I don't feel like it. I don't have patience. I know I'm getting better, but it's still frustrating when you have to rely on other people. You never have met a long hauler who got totally well. But I plan on being the first one. They had even told my wife to get ready to bury me in 2020 because I was so bad off.

The physical part of broadcasting even 50 games in 2021 was hard. The mental part was hard enough. But my broadcast partner John Rooney is so good. I can ask him any question on the air about a stat or something, which I wouldn't do to another broadcaster, but Rooney knows everything and he's so prepared. He's probably better prepared than any broadcaster in the history of the game.

If there was one regret I had in my final game, it was that I couldn't deliver my trademark call. By the time I finally slid into my broadcast chair in the bottom of the first, Tommy Edman was about to swing at Chicago righthander Alec Mills' first pitch and hit it over the right-field wall for the Cardinals' first run in what would become a 3–2 loss to the Cubs. "That [home run] was for you," Rooney said.

But it happened so fast that I didn't have a chance to say, "Get up, baby. Get up, baby! Oh yeah."

All through the season, people asked me to sign stuff, and I signed almost anything and everything. I owed them that for all they had done for me over the years.

One of the things I took out of this season is how good a job Mike Shildt, who got fired anyway, did managing his bullpen. It was as good as anybody I've ever seen. I was afraid they wouldn't be able to comb their hair by August. But not only could they comb their hair, but they also were effective the whole way. He did an unbelievable job. But believe it or not: closer Alex Reyes got him fired when he gave up that home run in the bottom of the ninth inning in the playoffs to the Los Angeles Dodgers. If Shildt wins that game, then they don't fire him.

Among other things I will be doing in the year ahead is getting another aortic valve for my heart. They said those only last 20 years, so I said I've got to get a new one, though I've only had this one for nine years. When I got my first valve operation, the doctor asked me where I was going to be on Monday. I said I was going to be in Chicago. She said, "No, you're going to be in the hospital for an operation."

A few days before that, I had passed out driving Lori's car. I ticked her off because while she was on the phone I ran over one of those little highway signs. I said, "If you weren't on the phone, you would have yelled sooner." That didn't go over too well with her, as you can imagine.

One thing I am proud of is I never swore on the air in my 50 years. One spring Whitey Herzog brought a preacher, reverend Bill Little, to camp. We had a bunch of milk drinkers on that club, and I guess Herzog was saying that instead of fighting them, he was going to join then.

Right when Little was getting ready to leave, Jack Buck asked the preacher what was the most surprising thing he saw that spring. He said, "Shannon talking off the air and on the air."

One of the best things that happened to me in my last year was something that didn't happen. Vin Scully, the great

Hall of Famer broadcaster of the Dodgers, said he wasn't going to vote for anybody until I was in the Hall of Fame. That was the biggest compliment I had.

But I didn't want to get overloaded with stuff in my last year. I told Lori to pretty much turn everything down. One of the places I did go to a lot was my restaurant up in Edwardsville, and people were always great, saying what a wonderful time they had listening and that they didn't want me to go. I didn't realize how important the broadcast was to baseball until about five years ago when people started coming up to me and saying things like that. They know they can trust me. One thing about it: if I say a pig weighs 39 pounds, they don't have to put it on a scale.

I traveled with the team for road games up to five or six years ago when I started doing mostly home games only. It was the right thing to do, but I missed seeing my friends— late night and otherwise—and the places we would go. Most of my friends on the road are dead now.

But it's time. Since I first got the COVID, it's been a real hard time. It is what it is. I use a cane now. I had a friend, whose mother had a cane but didn't use it, and she broke her hip and she died so I use the cane. And I fell down when I was hunting not long after I got out of the hospital. I wasn't supposed to be hunting that quickly. I still hunt. And I still play golf. I told Lori I could still beat her in golf, and she raised her eyebrows at that and said, "Sure you can."

I'm going to continue to play golf and hunt. My deer stand this last deer season was a mobile deer stand. It's a golf cart. My hunting buddies down in Kentucky fixed it up with camouflage and all that. It works. Somebody shot a turkey using it. They really take care of me.

In November, Lori and I got to fly on a private plane to Delmar Thoroughbred Club near San Diego for the Breeder's Cup races. And I won some money.

What I'm looking forward to is being able to do whatever I want whenever I want. I just want some time off, though I'm still going to go to spring training every year. But I'm finished broadcasting, where my motto all these years had been that I'm not going to think about what I'm going to say. I just say it.

This COVID really knocked the crap out of me, so it was hard. I got more tired. Like when I would do four games in a row, God, I'd get tired. I'm getting better and better, but I'm still way behind. I'm getting stronger, but people who don't take COVID seriously are wrong.

I feel fine, but I didn't realize how COVID could take advantage of you. I don't see any improvement in my energy. Lori sees improvement, but I don't. I guess I'm looking for bigger improvement. I want it to be all gone. What people think and what I think are two different things. What I think is the most important. I just know where I was and where I am now, and there's a large difference. I know in the long haul I'm going to come out on top, but I don't have patience. And you need patience.

I've still got my flip phone. They say it's indestructible. But nothing's indestructible, as far as I'm concerned.

People ask me if *Live at Shannon's* will be back on the radio after weekend games. It will probably be back, but I don't know for sure. We were talking about starting up another restaurant, but nothing is imminent right now. If we do get a place, though, those Friday and Saturday shows will be back. That's why I opened that place. I wanted to have a fine dining place after a game. And it turned out all right with *Live at Shannon's* becoming a product of that. You could say stuff at midnight that you couldn't say at 7:00 PM.

I'll still keep up with the game, though I'll probably listen to it more than I'll watch it, especially when we're down at the lakehouse in Marion, Illinois, where we spend most of our time now. We don't get the games on cable down there. I guess I could get it if I wanted. I'm not like Herzog, who watches all the baseball games and all the basketball games. He loves basketball. He said he'll fall asleep in his chair, and when he wakes up, he'll still be watching the same game, but it's a replay.

I'll come to the ballpark once in a while if they want me to sign autographs or something. But no more broadcasting. Lori's got some plans for me at the lake. She's having an outdoor pool put in and she says I've got to exercise. My golf game isn't quite the same in that I don't hit it as far as I used to, but I hit it straight. But I'm 82. So I get to tee off from the women's tees. I don't have to hit it as far. So maybe I can beat her.

There's a lot of good things and a lot of bad things that have happened. But we've conquered them, you know? What worries me is that I'm going to outlive my kids. I didn't worry about that until my two oldest boys turned 60. However, many in my family have lived a long time. I'm the oldest, but all my natural siblings—Kathy, Steve, Sharon, and Carol— are still alive.

I've lost a lot of great teammates in the past few years— Red Schoendienst, Bob Gibson, Lou Brock. But the one I miss the most is Roger Maris, who has been dead for more than 25 years. Boy, was he smart. He really knew the game. We had plenty of fun off the field, too. When I first came up, my roomie, Lew Burdette, paid for everything. He said, "You'll have your chance to do the same someday."

But I didn't have anybody I took under my wing when I got to be a veteran for the simple reason that nobody could hang with me—or they didn't want to take a chance. I told general manager Bing Devine that it wouldn't be fair to my roommate, whoever it would be. No. 1, I smoked. And No. 2, I like to get up early in the morning and order room service, where other guys like to sleep late.

I quit smoking all of a sudden after my house in Edwardsville burned down about 10 years ago because of faulty wiring. While the house was being rebuilt, I lived at the nearby Holiday Inn. I was smoking a lot, and it was hot. Every day it was about 110 degrees. It was uncomfortable. My wife tried to get me to stop smoking, and my kids tried to get me to stop smoking. They tried everything. They would even take off and leave me alone at the hotel, but it was uncomfortable enough at the hotel to make me quit. One day I just took the cigarettes and threw them out the window and said, "That's the last time I'll have a cigarette."

I was a big Marlboro and Salem smoker. I smoked since I was 12 years old. But there were a lot of pro athletes who were smokers when I played. Stan Musial smoked. Keith Hernandez and Ted Simmons were smokers. Tommy Herr was a smoker. When I played, about 50 percent of the players smoked. I'm sure it affected my play. I went for a stress test one time. The nurse asked me if I smoked and how many packs I smoked a day. And I said six or seven. She said, "What?"

I said, "You asked me, lady, and I told you."

The guys in the Hall of Fame probably all drank and smoked. But it was cool to do it in those days. Drinking and smoking were just part of the deal, and you hung around in places where they drank and smoked. The world is different nowadays. But if you make your mind up to do something—like stop smoking—you can do it. Players stopped smoking because of the education. We all smoked until we got educated. With all the advertisements about how injurious it is to your health, you'd have to be an idiot to smoke nowadays. Nicotine is more addictive than cocaine—or so I've heard from a guy down at the brewery who was lecturing us and who had tried them both. They say cigarettes are worse than marijuana, though I never tried marijuana.

Would I have done anything different in my life? Not really. I might have wished I played for a guy like Tony La Russa. He would have made me a better player. Herzog would have done that, too. But La Russa would have worked me differently.

I've always said I had nine lives and now I've used up two of them. Three, if you count that heart valve procedure I had a few years ago. But I have a distinct ability not to remember the bad things that have happened. The only thing I really missed out on was the football—because football came easily to me. I'll always wonder how good I might have been if I had played three years of college ball and then gone to the pros. But if I had done that, I wouldn't have hit a home run in each World Series I played in. Or broadcast Cardinals games for 50 years. And that's not too bad. Plus, I've got six or seven lives left to live.

JOHN ROONEY

I've worked with Mike since the 1980s on a part-time basis when I was still at Louisville and since 2006 together with him on the St. Louis Cardinals' network. It's been a good ride. We've had a lot of fun.

It's been tough on Mike the last year because of everything. All those different people he worked with in the booth when he started out—Jack Buck, Bob Starr, Jay Randolph, Dan Kelly—he had some pretty good people to learn from. But he never lost track of who he was—and I don't think he was capable of losing track of who he was. He's been involved with some real big hitters, but he was smart enough to know what to use and what not to. And just the rest of it came out. That's why I think he has some wide appeal. You don't know what he's going to say or when he's going to say it.

That stuff he said about the potential sale of the team, I got criticized because I didn't correct him. But what's to correct? I don't know it to be true or false. I don't know where he got it. You still have to be yourself. I think that's why he lasted 50 years.

Think of it: Mike's been there 50 years. He's the tie-in after losing Stan Musial, Red Schoendienst, Lou Brock, Bob Gibson, and several others over the years. That links a lot of Cardinals history that has touched so many people over the years. That's going to be one of the biggest differences.

Ricky Horton and I will bring a little something different along, but what we will bring along is what Mike taught both of us and Mike Claiborne and everybody else who's been in the booth. We're just there for a short time as caretakers in those chairs, but we have to show the respect for the game and give it everything we have like those in the past have done before us and what those should do long after we're not there. We want to have an entertaining broadcast and love what we're doing—because Mike loved everything he did. He lived life to the fullest more than anybody I know. And he enjoyed every minute of it.

There were times this past year when I know he was struggling, and I know he's a proud, brave man and wanted to push ahead and finish up what he started, and that's why we respect him for that. I respect him for the fact that I wouldn't be with the Cardinals if Mike didn't want me there. And I know that. We were able to form a pretty good team where Mike did his thing, I did my thing, and we brought it together. Mike liked the creativity. I thought Mike had some of his best years, going back to 2006 and from that point on. He did some unbelievable work in those world championship years, that's for sure.

I couldn't ask a lot of analysts or partners a lot of things I could throw at Mike, knowing what he's been through, what he's seen, what he's done. Even though he played far less than he broadcast in terms of years, he still had a lot of savvy. The thing about him is that Mike could see the field—whether it was football, baseball, or basketball, and that's what made him such a good athlete. He could read between the lines, and it was like, "Okay, I know what's happening next because I've seen this 100 times before."

He's lived it and the way he brought it to the Cardinals fans tied it all together. And he tied together a great baseball life. He's a competitive guy—whether it's hunting, playing cards, or if they have a roadblock up in front of the bus in San Francisco, he'll get out and move it. That's not going to stop Mike. He's going to get the job done no matter what it takes and he's going to have a pretty good time in the process.

For 50 years Cardinals fans got to enjoy that. People have asked me what kind of manager he would he have been. How would he deal with the players? I think he would be great. If Mike managed not long after he quit playing, I think he would have been fine because he can relate to people. He can sit down, talk to people, get the message across, and keep it in pretty simple terms when it comes right down to it. That's what he was able to do with Cardinals fans, and it's hard to do that on radio. It's easier trying to get across something as an analyst on TV. With those who can get that message across on radio, that can be very powerful and effective, and Mike did that.

His not being in the Hall of Fame is a crime. It's a shame because he sold more tickets and beer than anybody I know. I take a look at all those fans in the seats—all those two million to three million plus over the years of his career—as opposed to back in the '70s when we were over at the ballpark with 15 or 20,000 of our closest friends. This thing really started perking up after Whitey Herzog got there. It didn't let up much, and Mike was a major part of that.

Those beer distributors—and Mike knew them all—absolutely worshipped the ground he walked on. He would go into those communities in our Cardinals Network area and find ways to promote Budweiser— whether it was leaving the empty bottles on the table or going into a pub that wasn't serving Budweiser. When Mike got done, they were serving Budweiser. He wouldn't take no for an answer, and that's the way he was as a player, too. If something was going to beat him, he made sure it wasn't going to beat him for very long. For instance, the way he transitioned from the outfield to third base is one of the all timers. And if he had stayed healthy, he would have been a staple at third base, or they could have put him back in the outfield. He had one of the best arms I've ever seen. Incredible arm. Accurate and strong. And he knew where to throw. He knew the game and he knew it before he even got into the booth. He knew how to play.

For most of his broadcast career, Mike was down on the field. He was in the clubhouse. He was around it, and that's what was really different in the last two or three years. That was missing for all of us. Whether it was knowing about a player's family or whatever, that was his prep. He was the whole package. Mike Shannon loved every moment that he was at the ballpark.

And one thing we'll really miss is Mike's *Live at Shannon's,* and Mike used that same approach from those shows during rain delays in the booth. He was able to get things out of people, laugh at people. Some of the shows he did with Gibson or Ron Santo, or even generals like Franklin Hagenbeck or the late Hal Moore, or the stuff he got out of Tony La Russa were amazing. And the shows he did with Whitey Herzog were always great. That's where we've been so blessed. So many of these Hall of Famers and most of the players have stayed in the area and have been a part of Cardinals baseball for all those years. It means something to them. And don't think for a moment it didn't mean the same to Mike because that was his world.

There was no better baseball show out there than *Live at Shannon's*. You could set your watch by it on weekends. It had great stories and a lot of entertainment. People drove home with that thing on. We all had a front-row seat with Mike.

After the season, I hadn't seen him for a couple of months until the Missouri Sports Hall of Fame induction when he came to see Claiborne go in. We were at our table, and somebody said, "We're going to miss you."

And he said, "People are going to forget me."

He was joking around, but I said, "Mike, we won't let them forget you."

Forget Mike Shannon? That's not even borderline possible. That's completely impossible. That's an indelible mark. He didn't miss anything. They only made one Mike Shannon. Mike, this Bud's for you!

Acknowledgments

Rick Hummel and I had many enjoyable sessions discussing my life as an athlete and then my 50 years in the St. Louis Cardinals' broadcast booth, and he was there for all 50 of those years as he worked for the *St. Louis Post-Dispatch*. So I thank Rick and hope he had as good a time reliving memories as I did.

We both would like to thank the many sports and broadcast figures who added their sentiments about me in the book, including John Rooney, Bob Uecker, Vin Scully, Joe Buck, Bob Costas, Mike Claiborne, Tony La Russa, Bud Selig, Tim McCarver, Dal Maxvill, Joe West, and Dick Musial.

A tip of the cap also to our editor at Triumph Books, Jeff Fedotin. Thanks to the Cardinals Radio Network's Anne Carroll and to Ben Boyd, formerly of KMOX Radio and now with the Cardinals Network, for providing audio clips of some of my more memorable calls. And thanks to the Cardinals—from the DeWitt family to Dan Farrell and many others—not only for allowing me to broadcast their games for 50 seasons, but also for the organization's help in setting up the cover photo for the book, which was shot by Taka Yanagimoto. Thanks to my first broadcast partner, the late, great Jack Buck, for showing me the ropes in my new job.

Rick said he particularly wanted to credit the *Post-Dispatch* for archival help and to the Retrosheet website to backstop our recollections of particular plays, players, and games. In some cases, it was a good thing we double-checked them.

And none of this would have happened without the aid of my wife, Lori, who was a master at setting up schedules so Rick and I could get together often during the busy regular season to produce what we hope you had a good time reading, whether you laughed, cried, or just nodded your heads and smiled.

About the Authors

RICK HUMMEL has covered baseball for the *St. Louis Post-Dispatch* for 50 years. A former president of the Baseball Writers Association, he was honored by the National Baseball Hall of Fame in 2007 with the BBWAA Career Excellence Award. He also has been honored by the Missouri Sports Hall of Fame and the St. Louis Sports Hall of Fame. Hummel was coauthor of Hall of Fame manager Tony La Russa's acclaimed *One Last Strike*. He has three married children, Scott, Christy, and Lauren, and is married to Melissa, who has a married daughter, Camilla.

MIKE SHANNON broadcast St. Louis Cardinals baseball for 50 years before retiring after the 2021 season. Before that he was one of the most prominent three-sport athletes in St. Louis area high school annals and an outstanding freshman quarterback at the University of Missouri who went on to play baseball for the Cardinals. Shannon played in the majors for nine seasons before being forced to retire because of a kidney ailment in 1970. In that time he participated in three World Series, winning two and hitting a home run in each of the three World Series. A member of the Cardinals Hall of Fame, Shannon also has been honored by the Missouri Sports Hall of Fame, which gave him its Pinnacle Award in 2021. He is married to Lori and has six grown children: Michael, Timothy, Patricia, Peg, Daniel, and Erin.